£1·50

CHRISTIAN
MYSTICS
OF THE MIDDLE AGES
An Anthology of Writings

CHRISTIAN MYSTICS

OF THE MIDDLE AGES
An Anthology of Writings

Edited with an Introduction and
Biographical Notes by
Paul de Jaegher, S. J.

Translated by
Donald Attwater and Others

Dover Publications, Inc.
Mineola, New York

Bibliographical Note

This Dover edition, first published in 2004, is a republication of the first 177 pages of *An Anthology of Mysticism*, originally published by The Newman Press, Westminster, Maryland, in 1950.

Library of Congress Cataloging-in-Publication Data

Anthologie mystique. English. Selections.
  Christian mystics of the Middle Ages : an anthology of writings / edited with an introduction and biographical notes by Paul de Jaegher ; translated by Donald Attwater and others.
      p. cm.
  "A republication of the first 177 pages of An anthology of mysticism, originally published by The Newman Press, Westminster, Maryland, in 1950"— T.p. verso.
  ISBN 0-486-43659-4 (pbk.)
  1. Mysticism. I. Jaegher, Paul de. II. Attwater, Donald, 1892–1977. III. Title.

BV5082.3.A5813 2004
248.2'2—dc22

                                                              2004049311

Manufactured in the United States of America
Dover Publications, Inc., 31 East 2nd Street, Mineola, N.Y. 11501

CONTENTS

NOTE ON THE DOVER EDITION

This edition, which focuses on the great medieval mystics, does not include selections from the more recent writers (including Augustine Baker, Louis Lallemant, John Joseph Surin, John Peter de Caussade, Lucy Christine, and Gemma Galgani) who are mentioned in the editor's introduction on the following pages, "Why and How the Writings of the Mystics Should Be Read."

WHY AND HOW THE WRITINGS OF THE MYSTICS SHOULD BE READ

' I'M no mystic. Mysticism is not for the likes of me, but for the initiated.' That is the sort of answer one often gets—given quite genuinely and straightforwardly —from people, even people of undoubted spirituality, to whom one has recommended the reading of some mystical work. ' Perhaps . . . if they had an " unusual sort of soul " to be guided into the paths of perfection —but thank heaven Almighty God has spared them that responsibility.'

Such an answer is rather surprising in these days, for we are far from the time when readers of mystical books were few, and when indifference or even a certain suspicion hid much of the wondrous horizons of mysticism from man's eyes. During the past thirty years there has been a complete change : a flowering of mystical writing and of books about the mystics has appeared as if by magic, in many quarters coldness and distrust has given place to real enthusiasm, and periodical publications have been started with the object of giving a principal place to the study of mysticism. It cannot be denied that the reaction has even sometimes been excessive, wanting in prudence and discretion. Such enthusiasm would suggest that there is no need again to praise and recommend the mystical writers or to explain the

benefits to be derived from their works, but I nevertheless think it desirable to set down a few reflections on
these matters for the consideration of my readers.
For there are still dark places untouched by the
brilliant light of the revival of mysticism, there are
still those indifferent to the subject, above all, there are
still a number of spiritually-minded people who never
think of opening a book by a mystical writer. Plenty
of domestic libraries are well stocked with books of
devotion : but if you search the shelves for any works
of St. John of the Cross, of St. Teresa, of St. Angela
of Foligno, of Blessed Henry Suso, of the two Catherines,
of Richard Rolle, or of Augustine Baker, you won't
find them.

The objection alleged against reading these books
shows clearly that it is still opportune to try and dispel
prejudice against them, but I wish to be excused for
the present from replying to this objection, which I
will return to on a later page. Meanwhile I will set
out quite simply some of the benefits that accrue
from a reading of the mystics to all who want to make
spiritual progress ; the objection will then, I dare to
hope, vanish by itself.

To sum up : the good-willed and prudent reading of
mystical books can perfect our understanding by extend-
ing our knowledge of God and of spiritual things, and
as a natural consequence our will is kindled and
directed by the resulting desire for Him and His
service.

∞

Speaking in the first place of understanding, is it
not a law of love always to want to know the beloved
object better ? We cherish and are interested in
everything that enhances the quality of the loved one,
everything which shows us new aspects of him, everything that helps us to penetrate more deeply into his
soul. Understanding increases love and love needs

ever to grow, so it is always trying to feel the charms of the beloved in a new way.

If that is a characteristic of human friendship and love, then it will not be different with the love of God, and the truly Christian soul is always anxious to know more about the object of her love, God, and the country where He shall be possessed and enjoyed, Heaven. She loves God above all and more than herself, He is her sovereign preoccupation, and it is an ever new happiness to know more of Him.

Now God reveals Himself to us first analogically, in the beings that we live among. The thousand creatures whose variousness, beauty, and charms surround and attract us are only a pale reflection of the infinite loveableness of God. All that is beautiful, fine, good, lovely, is so simply and solely because God is beautiful, fine, good, lovely ; they are irradiated and made grateful to our eyes by a ray from His infinite perfections. Unhappily but few souls are habituated to looking beyond creatures to the Creator.

However, we have other than this analogical knowledge which tells us nothing, for example, of the mystery of the Holy Trinity. God Himself has come to our aid and unveiled to our faith the truths of the three Divine Persons, His love for us, and its grand manifestations : the Incarnation, the Redemption, the Eucharist, the sojourn of God in the sanctified soul. He reveals Himself to us in the books of the Old Testament, which speak to us magnificently of God's power, wisdom, justice, loving-kindness, and mercy. The New Testament records the loveable virtues of the Word made flesh : the Gospels must always be the favourite book of a religious soul.

Then, to teach us yet more about God and His ways, we have the teachings of the saints. Those who left mystical writings especially tell us high things about God, His attributes, and His dwelling in the soul, about Heaven, our Lady, and the other holy ones, about all those unseen things of which we know so little and want to know so much. These privileged souls have come more close to God, and all that they can tell of their experiences to us other poor exiles is of endless interest and importance. Of course, even the mystics have not looked on the face of God in this life : what will be face-to-face in Heaven would be too blinding, too dazzling for us, dwellers of the night. The Bible tells us that no man can see God and live, and that is certainly true. But though they have not seen God they have been very near to Him, they have experienced Divine things, and felt the Divine presence. The Divine contact has inflamed them even to the depths of their souls. Without seeing God they have as it were caught a glimpse of Him as through a dazzling cloud—and they have been caught up in ecstasy.

What is ecstasy fundamentally if it is not the powerlessness of the body, unable to bear God's action and the delightful flame of His love? Ecstasy is the soul reaching her whole self out towards Him, recollected in all her powers, concentrating all her energies on giving herself to Him that she may enjoy and love Him wholly and freely; she is concerned only with God, drawn irresistibly by Him, trying, so to say, to get away from the earthly body that she may be made one with Him.

Even this brief and abstract reflection about ecstasy suggests much. It is moving to consider that upon the simple conscious approach of God, however closely hidden He may be, the soul is out of herself and the body becomes helpless before the onrush of spiritual desires and delights. The great human soul is infinite in its aspirations and never satisfied in this life by whatsoever multiplicity and attraction of things that seek to captivate it ; but at the merest hint of Divine contact she becomes still,

lost in praise and love, her cup of enjoyment overflowing.

If so much is called forth by a reference to
ecstasy in general terms, what is to be said of the
experiences which the mystics relate to us? 'Eye
hath not seen nor ear heard, neither hath it entered
into the heart of man, what things God hath prepared
for them that love Him!' exclaims St. Paul. This
ardent cry of the Apostle, suffering yet joyous in its
powerlessness, and magnificently eloquent in its bare
simplicity, has been echoed by all the mystics. St.
Ignatius Loyola cried out: 'How little worth appears
the world, when I look up to Heaven.' St. John of the
Cross, in a fine attempt to make us understand something of the Divine loveableness, said: 'If you had seen
a ray of my Well-beloved's glory you would be ready to
die a thousand times over to see it again; and when you
had seen it again you would be ready to die again to
see it again ...!' And St. Mary Magdalen dei
Pazzi, unable to control her love, burst out in sublime
frenzy: 'If a single drop of what I feel in my heart
fell into Hell, Hell would be straightway transformed
into Paradise!' These precious cries of the great
mystics, taken at random from their writings, are real
gems, and a little reflection on them will easily set our
hearts on fire.

The saints can only babble of what they have seen
of the Unseeable, understood of the Incomprehensible,
learned from the touch of the bodiless Spirit, but
these childlike babblings say more than the most
expert addresses. They touch us deeply, because
they are the result of the direct experience of men
like ourselves, who tell us, if I may put it so, about the
'reaction of the human soul' to the near approach of
her highest good and last end, God. We say instinc-
tively: 'Yes, indeed! If God had chosen me for
these Divine glimpses I too should have exulted in the
knowledge of an ecstasy of love. I have not seen God

and I know very little about Him, but this I do know, and this knowledge is more precious to me than the whole world—that the loveliness of God is such that should I see it clearly I should die of love : my soul would slip from my body to meet the embrace of her Well-beloved.'

∾

One of the principal reasons why so many genuinely religious folk make but little headway on the road to perfection is that their idea of God is too inadequate. Of course they know that He is without beginning or end, almighty, infinitely good and wise, but this knowledge is abstract, it is not ' lived.' All these formulæ are so cold : they really tell people very little and have even less effect on their hearts and actions than on their minds. Well, I know no better remedy for this than a careful and regular reading of the mystical authors.

The mystics will teach such people to conceive and realize God in a measure as they have realized Him themselves ; by meditation on their works He is brought down from His unattainable throne of glory to a tabernacle among men. Their pages speak of the Divine perfections in a way so concrete and actual, they are so overflowing with the God whom the writers have almost seen, warm and vibrant with the love that His loveliness has awakened in their hearts, that gradually these perfections become living and concrete to the reader, something that will be a powerful force in his life.

Open the book of the visions of Angela of Foligno anywhere and you will find invaluable pages about God, worth each one an entire treatise, and admirably apt to make us learn more interiorly His boundless love for His creatures or the height of His transcendence. Elsewhere she gives arresting descriptions of the action of God on the generous soul and the effects of His presence made sensible in her. She puts under our hand the idea of God's dwelling in the soul by sanctifying grace, an idea fundamental to Christian dogma and to the spiritual life. It is sometimes said that mystical experience is, as it were, sanctifying grace felt, made sensible, tangible, by the soul. It is right that more insistence should have been lately put on these great basic ideas of our religion, that efforts have been made to make us understand the nature of sanctifying grace and God's precious presence within us. And one of the best means to this end is to study, and recommend to others, the mystical writers.

Take St. Teresa of Avila. The whole of her spirituality is strongly imbued with this notion of the Divine dwelling in us : it is the very essence of her teaching, underlying every page she wrote. Her last and best work, *The Interior Castle*, is nothing else than a description of the wonders wrought by God in the soul He inhabits, wonders which contemplative prayer unfolds for us. She is always insisting on this idea, and often complains that her nuns in their prayers were too given to looking for God outside themselves in some far-away heaven, instead of embracing Him in their own hearts. Anyone who loves and uses the works of St. Teresa can hardly fail to get a grasp of this master idea, and by degrees to be drawn into loving and intimate converse with the in-dwelling God, which is perhaps the best preparation for an entry upon the ways of mysticism.

∞

At the same time as it gives a fuller and richer idea of God, reading of the mystics tends also to modify this knowledge by giving it something of that negative character which belongs to mystical contemplation.

It is well known that this contemplation becomes more negative the higher it advances, and the supreme understanding of God in this world is that which comes to the soul in what the pseudo-Areopagite calls ' the great darkness.'

We have no idea of what the mystic experiences during his union with God. The Divine loveliness acts upon him in a general and obscure way, but at the same time directly and so strongly that he can hardly bear the love which envelops him. But what affects him more than anything else is the clear perception that God is infinitely more than all that he can see or know ; however sublime and intoxicating his understanding may be, he knows that it is nothing beside the Divine reality. Or rather, this contrast is a part of his understanding : the certitude that ' God is not *that*,' or that He is that, but in a supereminent and incomprehensible way, is as it were its luminous halo. The mystic's knowledge of God and of His unutterable loveliness is shot through with this idea of Divine transcendence which is the foundation of mystical understanding and the source of its great value.

It has been rightly said that love goes further than knowledge, and St. Thomas Aquinas gives the reason : when it comes up against the unknown, which it can neither know nor understand, the mind stops and attempts no more ; will or love, on the contrary, goes ever on and upward. The lover does not love only what he knows of the beloved and has learned from time to time ; every day will show some new attraction or a new aspect of an old one : like an inexhaustible grain of radium, the hidden part of the beloved will continually unfold in some fresh activity or charm. So our will loves beyond our knowledge of the person loved, reaching out towards the treasury of still unseen qualities.

At first sight this seems out of accord with the axiom

according to which the will can follow blindly only the intelligence and cannot love a thing unless the intelligence has discerned it to be loveable. A thing is never loved except *sub ratione boni cogniti*, that is, for the good seen in it. But the difficulty is only apparent. There are two elements in all knowledge *that does not exhaust its object*. There is the positive element, the qualities actually perceived ; and the negative, the clear consciousness that our knowledge is not adequate, that the object loved is more and is worth more than we are able to see. The will goes beyond the positive element and finds a bridge across the gulf which separates us from the beloved and his ' complete knowability ' ; this bridge is precisely the negative element itself, that precious ' unknowingness,' as it has been called.

If knowledge of a beloved human has this character of negativeness and undefinedness, which acts as a spur to love, then how much more is this true of knowledge of God, the inexhaustible repository of truth Himself. The most ordinary Christian knows that God is infinite, and though the word may not mean much to us, generally only a bit of unmoving abstract information, still it has a certain real value for practical life ; and, to the extent that his knowledge of God extends and improves, its negative character increases and the whole becomes more valuable. Philosophers and theologians form in some way an idea of God by attributing to Him all perfections, all the beauties, all the charms that His creatures display, but with this clear and significant reservation, that they are in Him in a supereminent and trans-cendent way, in a mode of perfect simplicity which is infinitely beyond the grasp of created intelligence, whether human or angelic. His knowledge of God therefore is ' woolly,' indefinite, unfinished, and his understanding hands it on to his love as a treasure. The intelligence knows that it knows nothing, that its knowledge is immeasurably below reality, and it advises the will accordingly. This consciousness of its extreme insufficiency constitutes the most valuable part of his knowledge.

But, as I have said above, it is the mystic who is better equipped with this negative understanding than anybody else. Though for him the positive element exceeds the bounds of imagination, it is always surpassed and almost absorbed by the negative, the clear and lively consciousness of God's infinite transcendence. At the very moment when the ecstatic is out of himself with admiration and love, his understanding tells him that all he apprehends and sees is as nothing, absolutely nothing, in comparison with the unspeakable Reality. His shadowy knowledge is a cloud that is riven by momentary flashes of lightning. He thinks of the inexpressible transcendence of God, and of the complete inadequacy of his own comprehension of Him ; and in a flash, which may last for only a few moments, limitless distances of God's loveliness are opened to his mind.

That is the chief characteristic of the mystic's mysterious understanding of Divine things ; the further he goes towards God the wider horizons of unsuspected splendour he perceives, the more he is aware that there are others more magnificent yet to be discovered. Everything keeps on whispering to him : ' Higher, higher still ! God is yet more beautiful and enrapturing, He is infinitely other than the shadow that you see of His dazzling clarity. Never in this world will you know Him as He is, never will you taste of His perfections as they are worthy to be tasted ! '

Those of my readers who have some familiarity with mystical writings will have no need to verify what I have said. They know by experience that the reading of those works is calculated to enlarge our knowledge of God and to give it that negative character

which is emphasized by no one so strongly as by the
mystics.

∞

Since to read mystical books has on our knowledge
of God the effects I have just set out, it is only to be
expected that the will also should be strongly moved
and the conduct influenced by them. When we have
a more worthy idea of God, our love for Him becomes
greater ; when our understanding is enriched by the
knowledge of its own feebleness it will not cease to
urge our will, saying : ' Love ! love ever more, love as
much as you can, for God's loveableness is beyond all
love, and the marvels I have revealed are as nothing,
compared with the reality. Love then ; it is the only
thing you have to do on earth.' And the love-intoxicated
will echoes, ' Yes, love ! For you can never love
enough the God who is beyond the bounds of our
affections.'

The will is moved to reach out with all its strength
towards that One whom she knows so little, it becomes
obsessed by an unappeasable desire, a ceaseless need
to love God more and more. When she establishes
contact with the mystics the soul receives the wound
of love ; the shaft of Divine charity pierces it through
and through, leaving a gash that cannot heal : a
painful and yet thrice-loved wound. Henceforward
the soul has but one dream and aspiration, ever to see
a little more clearly and love more greatly Him whom
she knows so inadequately. She hungers and thirsts for
God and cannot be satisfied ; every thought, word,
and deed becomes simply a means of giving herself
more to Him and of making her offering of love less
unworthy of the ' too great Love.'

For another reason too, the reading of the mystics
is apt to enkindle our will and to inflame it with the
fire of Divine love. Mystical writings indeed are not
addressed exclusively to our minds ; their burning love

of God appeals directly to our hearts. The mystical
soul is enamoured of God, looks always towards Him,
lives in terms of Him because, in drawing near to
Divinity, she has consciously experienced, in that inner
depth where all her powers meet and matter is forgotten, 'essential love,' the innate love for God.

In truth, every soul desires God, her first object
and last end, but this love is generally unconscious.
'You made us for yourself, O Lord,' says St. Augustine,
'and our hearts can have no rest except in you.' The
rooted transcendental tendency is there in the soul,
but it has to be laid bare and brought into the consciousness ; the soul must experience and fully realize
the fact that she is 'in love' with God, that she longs
for the infinite Being and the supreme Good, and that
her insatiable desire for perfect happiness is actually
a desire for God.   Such discovery and experience
are beyond price and turn the soul in earnest towards
the heights ; but God grants these graces only to
those that are generous with Him.

By the touches of passive love which God bestows
on the mystics their souls become conscious, sometimes
little by little, sometimes all of a sudden, of their
essential 'native' love for God.   This love deepens
gradually, till it captures their whole existence and all
their life consists of giving way to this innate appetite,
this hunger for God which is now a part of their
consciousness and is even occasionally manifested to
the senses.

But the soul who has learned that she is made for
God, and that to live for and in union with Him is
her only wish, has ordinarily to undergo strange
sufferings.   She soon verifies for herself the word of
St. Augustine : *Quaeris fugientes te, fugis quaerentes te ;*
'O God, you seek those who hide from you, and hide
from those who seek you.'   God looks for the errant
sheep with tireless love and patience while it is wander-
ing among the thorns, but when the soul turns whole-

heartedly to Him the object of her love seems to avoid
her. To increase her desire God hides Himself from
time to time, and sometimes for long periods, and the
soul, wounded with Divine love, seeks agonizingly
for Him amid the night of passive purgation, knowing
sufferings of an intensity she has not before imagined.
At times it seems that God no longer loves her—and
why should He love a feeble creature stiff with pride
and selfishness? Despair lies in wait on anguish,
and the soul needs all her resources of faith and
confidence to continue to believe in spite of all in this
infinite Love she cannot find.

The writings of the mystics unfold for us the acts
and scenes of this touching love-drama, and there
is nothing so grand, so striking, or so instructive and
beneficial, as these mysterious alternations. As Emile
Baumann says: 'The most beautiful profane
romances are dull compared with the hidden lives
of the mystics and the books in which they recount
their experiences' (*L'anneau d'or des grands mystiques*,
p. 6). The most poignant things of life are nothing
beside a soul captivated little by little by the Infinite,
a helpless creature feeling itself now loved, now for-
saken, by eternal Beauty, the omnipotent King of
kings. For that is certainly one of the chief things
to be seen in the writings of the mystics, in the revelations of a Gertrude or an Angela, and in the ecstasies of
a Catherine of Siena or our nineteenth-century mystic,
Gemma Galgani. And to appreciate it there is not
the slightest need oneself to have received the great
mystical graces, visions or revelations, or to have
had a long initiation into the science of mysticism.
What *is* necessary is to love God a little and to want
to love Him more, and to feel sympathy with the noble
souls who in this life have talked intimately with
Him and experienced the unspeakable delights of
His embrace.

If we have a little of this love and sympathy we shall

profit immensely from reading the inner story of these
privileged souls and following the development of
the drama played out in their hearts, of which their
writings are the beneficent echo.   This can hardly
be done without emotion and without feeling in our
turn a spark of Divine love as we read the moving story
of which the Eternal Himself was in reality the author.
It is even possible that generous hearts studying in this
school will learn, under the influence of Divine grace,
to become conscious of the innate and essential love
of God which they have within them, and with the
aid of some mystical gift will become in their turn
souls completely enamoured of Him.

∽

The preceding pages have brought into relief one
of the most characteristic traits of mystical spirituality :
the huge predominance of God.   The mystic's soul is
full of God and absorbed in Him, wherefore in His
spirituality God is not just in the foreground, but is
all in all :   the ' I ' is only there in some way to point
the contrast.   *Noverim me, noverim te, oderim me, amem
te :* ' May I know myself and know you, O God, that
I may hate myself and love you,' says St. Augustine.
    The mystic's scorn of self is only the other side of
his love of God, its negative, downward, face.   To
love God is to give oneself up to looking at Him,
to contemplate Him with that prolonged, loving, and
' simple regard ' which is the occasion of the mystical
soul's passive love and sums up her prayer.   If from
time to time they look down towards themselves it is
in order that they may look up again with increased
longing and fervour to the unutterable Loveliness
who ravishes their souls.
    It is hardly necessary to emphasize how good a
spiritual trait this predominance of God is, and it
would be an incalculable gain were ' non-mystical '
souls and beginners in the mystic life to assimilate

it from the writings of the mystics. They are generous and whole-hearted in the fight against their faults and in the acquiring of virtue, but in a sense they are too preoccupied with themselves and their struggles, and so insufficiently conscious of God's love and loveliness ; they are more disgusted with themselves than appreciative of the Divine Beauty ; they do not think enough about losing themselves in God. Consequently their love of Him is without conviction and enthusiasm, and in moments of stress their self-centred virtue often fails.

Such people could profit much from the example of the mystics, who are oblivious of themselves because they love God so passionately ; the mountain air that blows across the uplands of their writings is the very cure for souls that are sick with self-examination and subtle egoism. In this clear atmosphere they can learn not only to fight self better than before, but also, and even more important, to disregard and forget self in contemplation of the perfections of God.

∞

There are other considerations which recommend the reading of the mystics, but it is sufficient to have indicated the part it may play in increasing understanding and love, and the gain to be had therefrom.

I have shown how such reading instructs us about God, His perfections, and our home in Heaven, and makes us participate after a fashion in the greater knowledge and experience which are the privileges of those chosen souls who have approached closest to God on earth. It can give us a more real and living idea of God and His attributes, of sanctifying grace, of the Divine dwelling in us, and so make our knowledge of these ill-understood matters less abstract and more fruitful. It also tends to impart to our knowledge of Divine things that eminent and negative element which is so valuable a characteristic of

mystical spirituality ; while at the same time our will
is enlivened and longs for a more burning love of
that God whom we know we can never love enough.
We are kindled by contact with these ardent souls
and by the dramas of Divine love which they so
poignantly describe for us.   Finally, their writings
are calculated to cure those souls whose spiritual life
is too subjective and involved with self ; their eyes
can be directed towards the loveliness of God, who
henceforward will hold the first place in their lives.

Now does all this presuppose a long and difficult
apprenticeship, unusual intelligence, or even certain
mystical gifts ?   Certainly not.   No such conditions
are required for us to learn to appreciate God and
His perfections and to acquire a more concrete and
living knowledge of Him from the mystics' magnificent
pages, any more than they are required for us to
catch some of the fire of the writers themselves.   The
only indispensable condition is to wish to know God
better and to love Him ever so little, sincerely wanting
to love Him more and more perfectly.   Obviously
there are obscure and difficult passages in mystical
books, sometimes many, sometimes only a few ; but
with these dispositions we shall always be able to
understand enough to enrich our knowledge and
intensify our love of God.

So you see how much is left of the objection, the
chief reason advanced against reading the mystics,
set out at the beginning of this introduction : ' I am
no mystic.   These doubtless excellent books were
not written for me.'

It can be answered with assurance : they were
written for you and for all other generous souls.
Provided you have the wish to know and love God
better, they will profit you, perhaps very much.
I willingly grant that such reading may be more
suitable for some sorts of mind or will than for others,
but that applies to all branches of human art and

science. It is none the less true that all can benefit from them. I will go further, and say that many people who judged themselves unsuited to tackle mystical books, and were persuaded to try, have been astonished to find how soon they were gazing at grand and unexpected vistas of beauty.

Of course it is desirable, in order to avoid disappointment or dangerous aberrations, to make a suitable and discreet choice at the beginning with the help of an experienced guide. To start off with Ruysbroeck or *The Living Flame of Love* would be to court discouragement and failure. But the treatise of St. Francis de Sales on the love of God or the writings of Fathers Surin, Lallemant, and Caussade, or of St. Catherine of Siena, or the memoirs of Sister Elizabeth of the Trinity, or the diary of Lucy Christine, or the shorter version of Dame Julian's ' shewings,' these can scarcely fail to attract and hold any and every generous soul.

With this reservation about a careful selection of books, I am convinced that a very large number of well-instructed religious people[1] who have never read a page of this kind would get nothing but good from the great mystics. It has been often said that St. Teresa won as many souls to God by her prayers and writings as St. Francis Xavier did by his preaching and miracles, and it certainly cannot be maintained that all who have benefited from reading St. Teresa were endowed with mystical graces. It is a pity that so many Christians ignorantly number themselves among those who think that ' it is no good for them to read St. Teresa ' and the other mystics. They should ponder the Church's prayer for her feast :

[1] To undertake mystical reading with confidence and the best results it is desirable first to be thoroughly conversant with the ascetical principles of the spiritual life, and to have practised them. See Garrigou-Lagrange : ' Ne pas brûler les étapes ' in *La Vie spirituelle*, 1930. To those who have some knowledge of the problems of mystical life I strongly recommend the *Etudes de théologie mystique*, by Père Joseph de Guibert, S.J. (Toulouse, 1930).

'Hear us, O God our saviour, that as we joyously celebrate the feast of Thy blessed maiden Teresa, so we may be fed with the food of her heavenly teaching and grow in loving devotion towards Thee.'

It is not superfluous to remark that the best fruits of mystical reading unquestionably accrue to those who have themselves taken the first steps in the mystical life ; such souls will more easily grasp the truths put before them, having already in some measure experienced them.

If, for example, God in His gratuitous goodness has occasionally given us some passing feeling of His presence, some glow of passive love, a sip, however short, of the ' prayer of quiet,' this reading will help us in some way to prolong those experiences ; it will make us appreciate at their real worth the graces which God may yet have in store for us and quicken our generosity towards Him. For, however far they may be from one another, the prayer of quiet, the prayer of rapture, and, highest of all, the prayer of transforming union are the same in kind. They are the stages in that contemplative prayer which consists, always and essentially, of a general, indistinct, and loving apprehension of God.[1]

It follows that a soul initiated by God Himself into the mysteries of the mystical life will appreciate the mystical writers more than another ; she will find a natural attraction in them and grasp their significance more readily.

Moreover, it is good that people should know something about the mystical life, for many stop short

---

[1] It must be remembered that mystical prayer and life in no way necessarily involve visions, ecstasies, rapts, and so on. They are accidental phenomena which sometimes accompany mystical union, especially in its intermediate stage, but they do not constitute it. They become rarer or stop entirely when the soul is completely purified and reaches the highest point of ' transforming union ' or spiritual marriage. I think it undesirable to multiply extracts bearing on these visions and ecstasies.

of the path of perfection because they do not realize or understand the ways along which the Divine Master would lead them. He visits them with the ' dark night of the senses ' and secretly changes their way of prayer in order to lead them from meditation to contemplation, but, lacking instruction and not suspecting Divine action, they persist in regretting the loss of their former way of prayer and active meditation. They struggle against God's intention and end by stopping where they are instead of going on to the higher degree of perfection that was open to them. If they had been ever so little acquainted with mystical things, enough to know at least that there is something other than meditation and a prayer full of visions, they would have gone much further on the road towards holiness.

I will say no more of this, but refer my readers, for more details, to St. John of the Cross.

∞

It is sometimes said that the books most read and enjoyed in these days are the best and the worst ; the most noble works are rivalled in popularity only by the most degrading and worthless. But it is surprising that while anthologies drawn from the works of profane writers are so numerous, those of religious literature are relatively few. I cannot think why, for there seem good reasons to believe that adequate anthologies of ascetical and mystical writing are welcome to the public.

In this volume, put together at odd moments stolen from active and laborious work, I have tried to set an example by filling a small part of the gap. I hope it will be followed by many other writers (and those, better qualified and with more leisure than myself), who will give us ' selections ' from religious works of all kinds.

After what I have said above it is not difficult to

see why I have given preference to an anthology drawn exclusively from mystical writers. Plenty of people have read ' devotional books ' who have never read ' mystical books.' It is my belief that an anthology that will give them an idea, however feeble, of what is to be found in such works will attract readers and encourage them to try the great mystics for themselves, seeking among them that increase of Divine love and knowledge which is their proper fruit.

Many and various considerations have governed the choice of extracts printed here, and it would be excessive to set them forth.[1] But I must say this much : Obviously it was not possible to give passages from all the mystics in a single volume ; I have preferred to give several and fairly long extracts from each of a few writers, lack of space necessitating the omission of several important ones. Moreover, as this is a ' popular ' work, intended for readers who mostly have little or no knowledge of mysticism, I have had most regretfully to leave out the finest passages of the authors quoted. They are too high and difficult, especially out of their context, to be suitable for readers who have no special preparation for them. This collection then must be regarded as ' selected passages ' rather than as ' the finest passages ' from the mystics. The extracts have also been chosen generally with an eye to illustrating the characteristic manner of the writer concerned.

I pray that this modest collection may fulfil its object of suggesting to people the beauties which lie hidden in mystical books, and that they may thereby be led to a greater knowledge and love of the God whom the mystics loved so much ; but even were we to love Him as much as they did we should still not love Him so much as He should be loved.

P. DE JAEGHER, S.J.

---

[1] The extracts given are only from authors who wrote in modern languages.

ST. ANGELA OF FOLIGNO

1248—1309

ANGELA was married to an Umbrian nobleman, by whom she had several children, but gave herself to a disorderly life, during which she lost her husband and children as well as her own innocence. She was recalled to penitence and vowed herself to a life of poverty and care of the sick as a Franciscan tertiary.

Like all the other great mystics, Angela underwent terrible trials in the ' dark night of the spirit,' which lasted two years. Nor was she spared the attacks of evil spirits and of temptations to sensuality so violent that she would counteract them by applying fire to her flesh, until her confessor, Friar Arnold, forbade. Her sufferings were followed by many mystical graces. Our Lord signed her with the ring and cross of His love, and she heard Him call her ' His dearest child of any in the valley of Spoleto.' St. Angela exercised a strong attraction over her contemporaries, and there gathered round her a band of men and women whom she directed in spiritual and corporal works.

The words she uttered in ecstasy were written down by Friar Arnold, and they are unsurpassed in their kind, opening out for the sympathetic reader a view of those heavenly joys which are the future lot of those who on earth lovingly lose themselves in the arms of God.

WORKS : *The Divine Consolation of Blessed Angela of Foligno* (Chatto and Windus, 1909).

A critical edition of the works of St. Angela has been made by Father Doncœur, S.J.

THE FEARFUL NIGHT OF THE SOUL

ANGELA experienced two years of those cleansing sufferings whereby God purifies the soul from the smallest faults and leads her on to perfect union. This is what St. John of the Cross calls ' the dark night of the soul,' and Angela describes it thus :

In order, therefore, that I might not feel myself exalted by the magnitude and the number of the revelations, visions, and conversings with God, and that I might not be puffed up with the delight thereof, the great tempter was sent unto me, who did afflict me with many and divers temptations, wherefore was I afflicted both in my soul and in my body. The torments of the body were verily numberless and were administered by many demons in divers ways, so that I do scarce believe that the sufferings and infirmity of my body could be written down. There remained not one of my members the which was not grievously tormented ; neither was I ever without pain, without infirmity, or without weariness. Always was I weak and feeble, and full of pain, so that I was compelled to be almost continually lying down. All my limbs were as though beaten, and with many troubles did the demons afflict me. Thus was I perpetually sick and swelled, and in all my limbs I did suffer pain, so that it was difficult for me to move myself. Nevertheless, was I not weary of lying still, neither was I yet able to eat sufficient. In short, the sufferings of the body were great, but those of the soul were beyond all comparison, more bitter and more numerous, and all were inflicted by the same demons. I can only liken myself unto one who is hanged by the neck, his hands tied behind his back and his eyes bound, and who is left hanging by a rope upon the gallows ; and although he hath no help or remedy or support, he doth, nevertheless, continue to live in that torment and cannot die. And I do affirm that even more desperately, and with greater cruelty was I afflicted by demons, for they hanged my soul and all its strength was overwhelmed and departed from it. And seeing how that I had no power to oppose them, my grief was so great that at times I was scarce able to weep for rage and for grievous suffering. Moreover, I wept without obtaining relief, and ofttimes was my rage so great that I could scarce refrain from rending myself and beating myself most grievously, thus causing my head and all my members to swell. When my soul beheld itself cast down and all its virtue departed from it, then it made great lamentation, and then did I cry unto my God.

After this I did endure another torment, for every vice was re-awakened within me. Not that—albeit re-awakened—they had power to overcome my reason, but they did occasion me much tribulation. And not only did I remember those vices which assailed me in times past, but many others which I did never before know entered into my body and did inflame me and cause me the utmost suffering. But because they had no lasting power over me they did afford me great consolation when they began to weaken and leave me. This was the work of the demons into whose hands I perceived I had been delivered, but when I do remember how that God was afflicted here below and in poverty, I would that mine own sufferings might be increased twofold.

At times was I thrown into a most horrible darkness of spirit by the demons, wherein it did appear that all hope of good was withdrawn from me. Then those vices which were dead inwardly in the soul were revived outwardly in the body, both those which I did never before feel, and those which I did have aforetimes. And I did suffer so greatly that I was constrained to put actual fire upon my body in order that it might quench the burning of desire ; and this I did continue to do until my confessor forbade me. And when I was in that darkness of spirit methought I would have chosen rather to be roasted than to endure such pains. Wherefore did I cry aloud and call upon death, desiring that it should come in any form whatsoever if only God would permit me to die.

And unto God did I say : ' Lord, if Thou wilt send
me into hell, I pray Thee tarry not, but do it instantly,
and since Thou hast abandoned me, make an end of
it now and plunge me into the depths.' Presently
I perceived that this was the work of demons and that
such vices exist not in the soul, for never would I have
consented thereto. Howsoever, the body doth suffer
violence, and so great is the grief and pain that if it
should endure the body would not be able to bear
it. Moreover, the soul doth find that all its strength
hath been taken from it, and albeit it doth in no wise
consent unto vice, yet can it not resist. And seeing
that it doth act contrary to the will of God, it loseth
all hope of being able to resist and is tormented by
those vices.

Among others, God did permit one vice to enter into
me the which I had never before known, but I did
clearly perceive that it entered into me by Divine
permission, and it was so great that it did exceed all
others. Upon the other hand was there given unto
me a certain virtue, manifestly wherewith to oppose
the aforesaid vice and by means of which God did
most potently set me free. Wherefore even if I had
not already possessed a sure faith in God, this one
thing alone would have inspired me with such a faith
and a certain hope, of the which I could in no wise
doubt. For virtue did increase and vice did diminish,
and I was so upheld by that virtue that I could not
consent unto wrong-doing, and likewise by means of
that virtue was I so enlightened and strengthened
that not all the men who were in the world, nor all
the demons, could have persuaded me to commit
the smallest sin. Hence proceedeth the aforesaid
faith in God. The aforesaid vice was so great that I
am ashamed to speak of it, and of such potency that
if the virtue had tarried in coming to succour me,
neither shame nor suffering nor any other thing
whatsoever would have sufficed to restrain me from

instantly falling back into sin. And all this did I bear for the space of more than two years.

A PILGRIMAGE TO ASSISI

FEW descriptions of God's boundless tenderness towards the loving soul equal the following :

Now when I was come to that place which lieth between Spello and the narrow road which leadeth upward unto Assisi, and is beyond Spello, it was said unto me :

' Thou has prayed unto My servant Francis, and I have not willed to send thee another messenger. I am the Holy Spirit, who am come unto thee to bring thee such consolation as thou hast never before tasted. And I will go with thee even unto Saint Francis ; I shall be within thee and but few of those who are with thee will perceive it. I will bear thee company and will speak with thee all the way ; I will make no end to My speaking and thou wilt not be able to attend unto any save unto Me, for I have bound thee and will not depart from thee until thou comest for the second time unto Saint Francis. Then will I depart from thee in so far as this present consolation is concerned, but in no other manner will I ever leave thee, and thou shalt love Me.'

Then began He to speak the following words unto me, which did persuade me to love after this manner :

' My daughter who art sweet unto Me, my daughter who art My temple ; My beloved daughter, do thou love Me, for I do greatly love thee and much more than thou lovest Me.' And very often did He say unto me : ' Bride and daughter, sweet art thou unto Me, I love thee better than any other who is in the valley of Spoleto. Forasmuch as I have rested and reposed in thee, do thou also rest thyself and repose in Me. I have been with the apostles, who did behold

Me with their bodily eyes, but they did not feel Me as thou feelest Me. When thou shalt be come unto thine house thou shalt feel another sweetness, such as thou hast never yet experienced. I shall not speak unto thee as I now speak, but thou wilt only feel Me. Thou hast prayed unto My servant Francis, hoping with him and through him to obtain the things thou desirest, seeing that as My servant Francis hath greatly loved Me, I have done many things for him. If there were to-day any person who loved Me more, much more would I do for him.'

Then said He unto me that there are few good persons in these days and but little faith, for which cause He did lament, saying, ' So great is the love of the soul who loveth Me without sin, that, if there were any one who loved Me perfectly, I would show him greater mercy than I have ever shown hitherto, and thou knowest that many great things are recorded which I have done unto divers persons in times past.'

None can excuse themselves for not having this love, because it is possible for all persons to love God, and He asketh nothing save that the soul shall love and seek Him. He is the love of the soul. But these are deep sayings.

That God is the love of the soul did He set forth unto me with lively proof, by His advent and His Cross borne for us, albeit He was so great and glorious. And He did expound unto me His Passion and the other things which He did for our sake ; then He did add, ' Behold now, if there be aught in Me save love.' He did grieve for that in these times He could find no person upon whom He could pour out His grace, and He did repeat that He would show far greater mercy unto whosoever should love Him at this present time than He had shown unto the saints and the blessed ones hitherto.

Then did He begin again to say unto me, ' My beloved daughter who is sweet unto Me, love thou

Me, for I do love thee more than thou lovest Me.
Love Me, My beloved, for boundless is the love
which I bear unto the soul who loveth Me without
any sin.' Methought He did desire to be loved with
that same love which He bore unto the soul, according
unto the power and virtue of the soul, and that if
only the soul itself would desire this, He would bring
it to pass.

Again He said unto me, ' My beloved and My
bride, love thou Me ! All thy life, thy eating and
drinking and sleeping and all that thou dost is pleasing
unto Me, if only thou lovest Me.' And He said,
' I will do great things through thee in the sight of all
people ; thou shalt be known and glorified, so that
many shall praise My name in thee.'

These and other similar things did He say unto me.
Then, when I heard these words I did count over my
sins and consider my faults, and how that I was not
worthy of such great love. And I did begin to cast
doubt upon these words, wherefore my soul said unto
Him who had spoken unto it : ' If Thou wert truly
the Holy Spirit Thou wouldst not speak thus unto me,
for it is neither right nor seemly, seeing how that I am
weak and frail and might grow vainglorious thereat.'

He answered me, ' Reflect and see if thou couldst
be vainglorious because of all these things for the
which thou art now grown proud ; and see if thou
couldst not perceive the folly of thy words by thinking
of other things.'

So then did I endeavour to grow vainglorious,
that I might prove if what He had said were true ;
and I began to gaze at the vineyards, that I might
learn the folly of my words. And wheresoever I
looked He said unto me, ' Behold and see, this is
My creation,' and thereat did I feel the most ineffable
sweetness.

THE BEAUTY OF GOD

Upon a certain time when I was at prayer and my spirit was exalted, God spake unto me many gracious words full of love.

And when I looked, I beheld God who spake with me. But if thou seekest to know that which I beheld, I can tell thee nothing, save that I beheld a fullness and a clearness, and felt them within me so abundantly that I can in no wise describe it, nor give any likeness thereof. For what I beheld was not corporal, but as though it were in heaven. Thus I beheld a beauty so great that I can say naught concerning it, save that I saw the Supreme Beauty, containeth within Itself all goodness. And all the saints were standing before this beauteous Majesty, praising it.

Methought, however, that I stayed in this trance but a very brief while; then said God unto me, 'My beloved daughter, dear unto Me, all the saints of Paradise do bear an especial love toward thee, and likewise doth My mother, and they will bring thee unto Me.' And albeit these words were spoken unto me, all concerning His mother and all the saints seemed unto me but a small thing. For so great was my joy in Him that I took no heed of looking at the angels and the saints, because all their goodness and all their beauty was from Him and in Him; He was the whole and Supreme Good, with all beauty, and so great a joy had I in His words that I paid no heed to any creature.

Again He said unto me, 'Infinite is the love which I bear thee, but I do not reveal it unto thee—yea, I do even conceal it.'

Then answered my soul, 'Wherefore hast Thou such love and joy in me, who am hateful, inasmuch as I have offended Thee all the days of my life?'

To this did He make answer, 'So great is the love

I bear thee that I no more remember thy sins, albeit
Mine eyes do see them ; for in thee have I much
treasure.'

Then did my soul feel an assurance so true that it
doubted no more. It felt and saw that the eyes of
God were searching within it, and it had such joy in
those eyes that neither man nor saint come down
from heaven could declare it. When He told me
that He concealed much love, because I was not
able to bear it, my soul answered : ' If Thou art God
omnipotent, make Thou me able to bear it.'

Then He made answer finally and said : ' If I
were to do as thou askest, thou wouldst have here all
that thou desirest, and wouldst no longer hunger
after Me. For this reason will I not grant thy request,
for I desire that in this world thou shouldst hunger
and long after Me and shouldst ever be eager to find
Me.'

THE UNUTTERABLE

WHEN He presenteth Himself unto the soul He doth
reveal and make Himself manifest, and doth thus
enlarge it to receive gifts and sweetness never known
before and greater and deeper than hath been
described.

Unto the soul (not drawn forth out of all darkness)
is then vouchsafed the utmost knowledge of God
which I do think could be granted. And it is given
with so much clearness, sweetness, and certainty,
and hath such depth, that the human heart cannot
attain unto it, nor can my heart ever return again
to the understanding and knowledge thereof, or to the
imagining of aught regarding it, saving only when the
supreme God doth vouchsafe unto the soul to be
exalted even unto that which the heart can no more
reach. Therefore is it not possible to say anything
whatsoever concerning it, or to find words wherewith

to express it; neither can the imagination or the understanding in any way reach unto it, so immeasurably doth it exceed all things.

Thus do we perceive that by nothing that we can think or say can God be exalted. The Holy Scriptures are so far above us that no man—be he the wisest in all the world and possessing all the knowledge it is possible to have in this life—can fully and perfectly know and understand them; there is none whose intelligence would not be always overcome by them. Of these most excellent and divine workings in the soul whereby God doth manifest Himself, can man in no wise speak or even stammer. But inasmuch as my soul is oft-times uplifted to know the Divine secrets, I do understand wherefore the Holy Scriptures were written, what they do appear to affirm and deny, that which is easy and that which is difficult, and why some derive no profit from them, and why those who do not observe them are condemned and those who do observe them are saved by them. Thus have I an advantage in knowing these things, and after learning the secrets of God I can speak some few words with certainty; yet are my words outside of those divine and ineffable workings, and in no way do they approach nigh unto them, but rather do they spoil and blaspheme, as I have always said.

Therefore do I say that if all Divine consolations, all spiritual joys, all heavenly delights which ever were in this world—if all the saints who have lived from the beginning of the world until now were to expound and show forth God, if all the worldly delights, both good and evil, which ever existed were all to be converted into one good and spiritual joy which should endure until I were made perfect, I would not, even that I might obtain all this, give or exchange even for the space of the twinkling of an eye that joy which I have in the unspeakable manifestation of God.

DIVINE CONFIRMATION

GOD spoke to the soul of Angela, who asked for a sign that it was really the Divine voice she heard. It was given.

Upon another occasion whilst I was at prayer, exceeding pleasant words were spoken unto me after this manner :

' O, My daughter, who art far sweeter unto Me than I am unto thee ; thou art the temple of My delight, and the heart of the Omnipotent God resteth upon my heart.'

Together with these words there came upon me a feeling of the utmost joy, such as I had never before experienced, inasmuch as all the members of my body felt it. And as I did prostrate myself at these words, it was further told me :

' The Omnipotent God loveth thee more dearly than any other woman of this city. He rejoiceth in thee and in thy companion. Do ye both strive, therefore, that your lives be as a light unto all who desire to follow your example ; but unto those who follow you not, shall your lives be as a judgement strict and hard.'

My soul did here understand that this cruel judgement was pronounced against the learned rather than against the laity, because they do despise these heavenly things by reason of knowing them in the Scriptures. Yet was I told that so great was the love which Almighty God bare unto us that He was continually with us, albeit not with these feelings. And I was told that His eyes were now upon us ; whereupon methought that I beheld His Divine eyes with the eyes of my mind, and I rejoiced more than I can say. Nevertheless, I do grieve because the words we are now saying are so unworthy.

Albeit I had great joy of this matter, yet did I

remember my sins and I did esteem that neither now or at any time had there been in me any good which might be pleasing unto God. Wherefore began I to doubt, seeing that great things had been spoken unto me ; and I said :

' If Thou who speakest unto me wert truly the Son of Almighty God, my soul would feel a joy higher and greater than this, and I should not be able to bear it, feeling that Thou wert in me, who am so unworthy.'

Unto this He made answer, ' I desire not that thou shouldst have a greater or more perfect joy than this at the present time, but I have prepared a greater one for thee. Thou must know that the whole world is full of Me.'

And verily I did then perceive that every creature was full of Him. Again He spake unto me, saying, ' I can do all things, I can make thee to see Me as when I talked with My disciples and yet to feel Me not.'

This was not said unto me in actual words, but my soul comprehended that which He said, and many things greater still, and thus it felt them to be true. Yet in order to be clear whether that which was said was verily true, my soul cried :

' Forasmuch as Thou art Almighty God and the things Thou tellest me are true, give Thou me a sign whereby I may be sure thereof, and release me from this great doubt.'

Then I besought Him that He would give me some tangible sign, something which I could see ; such as putting a candle into my hand, or a precious stone, or some other thing, or that He would give me any sign He pleased, promising Him that I would show it unto no person save unto whom He should desire. Then He replied :

' This sign that thou seekest is one that would only give thee great joy when thou didst behold or touch it, but it would not free thee from doubt, and thou

mightest be deceived by that sign. Therefore will I
give thee another sign, better than the one thou seekest,
and which will be for ever with thee, and in thy soul
thou shalt always feel it. The sign shall be this :
thou shalt be ever fervent in love, and the love and
the enlightened knowledge of God shall be ever with
thee and in thee. This shall be a certain sign unto
thee that I am He, because none save I can do this.
And this is a sign which I will leave in thy soul, the
which is better for thee than that which thou didst
ask of Me. My love do I leave in thee, so that for love
of Me thou wilt endure tribulations, and if any person
speak or do evil unto thee thou wilt be grateful,
declaring thyself unworthy of so much mercy. Such
is the love which I bare unto you all, for whose sake
I patiently and humbly endured all things. Thus
thou shalt know whether or not I am in thee if, when
any person shall speak or do evil unto thee, thou art
not only patient, but even desirous that they should
hurt thee and be grateful unto them. And this is a
certain sign of the grace of God. And behold, I do
now anoint thee with an ointment wherewith a
saint called Siricus and many other saints were
anointed.'

Then did I immediately feel that ointment, and so
sweet was it that I longed for death, and that I might
die with all manner of bodily torments. The torments
suffered by the martyrs who had died for Christ did
I esteem as naught, and I desired that for love of Him
my torments should be more terrible than theirs,
and that the world should cry out upon me with
insults and revilings.

Moreover, I rejoiced greatly in praying for those who
might work me these evils, and I marvelled not at the
saints who prayed for their murderers and persecutors ;
for not only ought we to pray unto God for them, but
we should beseech Him to grant them especial grace.
Therefore was I very ready to pray for those who did

me evil, to love them with a great love, and to take
compassion upon them. In that anointing I did
feel such sweetness both within and without that
I never felt the like before, and I have no words
wherewith I can show forth the least part of it.

This consolation was different, and of a nature
unlike the others. For in the others I had desired
immediately to quit this world, but in this my desire
was that my death should be grievous and prolonged,
with all manner of torments, and that my members
should suffer all the tortures of the world. Yet all
this seemed but a small thing unto me, for my soul
knew well that every torment was but a small thing in
comparison with the blessings promised in the life
eternal. My soul knew of a certainty that it was thus,
and if all the wise men of the world had told me the
contrary, I should not have believed them. And if
I should swear that all who walked upon the aforesaid
way would be saved, I should believe that I spake the
truth.

This sign did God leave so firmly implanted in
my soul, with so bright and clear a light, that me-
thinketh I could endure any martyrdom. This sign,
moreover, leadeth continually upon the straight way
of salvation, that is to say, it leadeth unto love and the
desire to suffer for love of God.

Moreover, I heard the words which God spake unto
me, saying, ' At the end of these things shalt thou cause
to be written, " Unto God be the thanks," and whoso
desireth to keep the grace which he hath shall not turn
his eyes away from the cross, whether it be joy or
sorrow that I do send upon him.'

All these aforesaid things concerning this sign did
my soul comprehend much more fully than I can
explain, and with a completeness whereby I was
enabled to understand many more things than I have
told here. My love and joy was so great that I can
in no wise express it, and may God not impute it

unto me for a sin that I have related all this with so many faults and shortcomings.

TRUE AND FALSE LOVE

ANGELA contrasts God's great love for her with her imperfect love for Him.

Upon the fourth day of the great week I was meditating with grief upon the death of the Son of God, striving to empty my mind of all other things in order that my soul might be the more absorbed in this Passion and Death.

Being, therefore, wholly occupied with the endeavour and desire to cast out every other matter from my mind in order that I might the more speedily and completely think only upon this, I heard the Divine voice saying within my soul, ' My love for thee was no deceit.' This word was as a shock of mortal pain unto my soul, for the eyes of my mind were instantly opened, and I saw that what He said was very true. I saw the working and effect of that delight ; I saw all that the Son of God had done for the sake of this love, and I saw what Christ Crucified had borne in life and in death for the sake of this deep and unspeakable love. Wherefore did I understand that it was indeed true that His love for me had been no deceit or jest, but love most perfect and profound. Then did I perceive just the opposite in myself, that is to say, I knew that I loved Him deceitfully and not truly. For this reason did I suffer such mortal pain and intolerable grief that methought I was about to die.

Then were other words spoken unto me, which did make mine anguish greater still ; and the words were these :

' Again I say unto thee, My love for thee was no deceit, My service of thee was not feigned, nor was My feeling for thee one of enlargement.'

Then cried my soul, saying, ' O, Master, that
which Thou sayest is not in Thee, is wholly in me ;
for never have I loved Thee saving deceitfully. I have
served Thee with lies and I have never desired to
draw nigh unto Thee in very truth for fear lest I
might feel those burdens which Thou didst feel and
bear for my sake. Wherefore have I never served
Thee sincerely and for Thine own sake, but with
negligence and duplicity.'

Now when I perceived how that He had loved me
sincerely, how that He bore in Him all the signs of
true love, and how that He had drawn nigh unto me
to such a degree that He was become Man in order
that He might more completely bear and feel in
Himself all our sufferings, I did feel such exceeding
great anguish that my ribs seemed disjointed and
methought mine heart would burst asunder. Reflect-
ing, moreover, upon these words, ' My feeling for
thee was not one of enlargement,' I did hear Him
say further unto me, ' I know thy soul more intimately
than it knoweth itself,' and these words did increase
mine anguish, inasmuch as the more I perceived how
intimately God did know me, the more did I realize
that I myself had become enlarged.

After this He spake certain words unto me which I
did manifest and show forth His boundless love,
saying :

' If there were any person who desired to feel Me
in his mind, I would not withdraw Myself from him ;
and unto whomsoever did desire to behold Me would
I willingly show Myself and with whomsoever did
desire to speak unto Me would I joyfully converse.'

These words did arouse in me the desire never to
feel or say or do aught which should offend God.
And this is what God desireth and especially seeketh
in His sons and His elect ; for He hath called and
chosen them in order that they think, see, and speak
according unto His will, and that they may take

heed to do nothing contrary thereunto. Thus was it set forth and told unto me :

' Those who love My poverty, suffering, and contempt are My lawful sons and Mine elect, whose thoughts are fixed on My Passion and Death, for here and nowhere else is found salvation and true life for all ; wherefore are these and none other My lawful sons.'

JESUS SUFFERED FOR ME

WHEREFORE, hearing what had been said, the soul did instantly endeavour to show forth all the sins which it had committed with the different members of the body and with all its own strength and powers, saying :

' O, Lord, Master and Physician of eternal health ! O, my God, forasmuch as by only showing forth unto Thee my infirmities and diseases Thou has consented to heal me, and because, oh Lord, I am very sick and have no part in me that is not corrupt and defiled, I, wretched that I am, will show Thee, O Lord, all mine infirmities and all the sins of all my members and of all the parts of my soul and body !'

Then did I begin and point them all out, saying, ' O Lord, most merciful Physician, look upon mine head and see how oft-times I have adorned it with the emblems of pride, how I have many times deformed it by curling and braiding my hair, and have committed numerous other sins. Look, O Lord, upon my wretched eyes, full of uncleanness and envy !'

In like manner I strove to number and show forth all the sins of mine other members. And when He had hearkened thereunto with great patience, the Lord Jesus Christ did gladly and joyfully make answer that He had healed these things one after another—and then, taking pity upon my soul, He said :

' Fear not, My daughter, neither do thou despair ;

for even wert thou tainted with a thousand deadly diseases, wert thou dead a thousand times, yet could I give thee a medicine whereby thou mightest be healed of everything if thou wouldst only apply it unto thy heart and soul.   For the infirmities of thine head which thou has told and shown unto Me, and for which thou art displeasing unto God and grievous unto thyself, which infirmities thou has incurred by washing, combing, anointing, colouring, adorning, and braiding thy hair, by setting thyself up in pride and seeking vainglory, for which things thou didst deserve to be cast into the uttermost parts of hell, to be humbled in all eternity and reputed as one most vile, for these infirmities have I given satisfaction and done penance.   I suffered the most grievous pain inasmuch as My hair was plucked out and My head pierced by sharp thorns ; with a rod was it smitten and covered with blood, it endured all manner of mockery and scorn, and with the vilest of crowns was it crowned.

' For the infirmity of thy face, which thou hast contracted likewise by washing and anointing it, by showing it unto miserable men and seeking their favour, I have made and ordained a medicine.   For these sins have I also given satisfaction, for wicked men did spit in My Face, making it all filthy and stained ; it was swollen and deformed by rude and heavy blows and a vile cloth was hung before it.

' Moreover, for thine eyes, with which thou hast looked at vain and hurtful things and hast delighted in gazing at many things which were opposed unto God, have I given satisfaction, shedding copious and bitter tears from My eyes which were veiled and filled with blood.

' For the ears wherewith thou hast offended God by hearkening unto vain and hurtful things and taking delight therein, I have done great penance, hearkening unto many grievous things, such as false accusations, slanders, insults, curses, mockings, lies and blasphemies, and finally the wicked judgement spoken against Myself—but above all I did penance in hearkening unto the weepings of My most loving and lowly mother, who grieved for Me with exceeding great grief.

'Because of the sins of thy mouth and throat, wherewith thou didst take delight in feasting and drunkenness and in the sweetness of delicate meats, My mouth hath been dry and empty, hungry and thirsty, it had fasted and been made bitter with vinegar mingled with gall.

'For the sins of thy tongue, which thou hast let loose in slanders, calumnies, derisions, blasphemies, lies, perjuries, and other sins, I did shut My mouth in the presence of judges and false witnesses, no excuses issued from My mouth, and with all Mine heart did I pray unto God for those who did Me evil, and I always preached the truth.

'Because of the sins of thy power of smell, whereby thou didst delight in flowers, I did smell the abominable spittle which I endured upon My face and eyes and nostrils.

'For the sins committed with thy neck, by shaking it in anger, pride, and lasciviousness, and against the Supreme God, I suffered many and divers blows upon My neck.

'For the sins of thy shoulders and back, whereby thou hast offended in bearing many things which were opposed unto God, I did penance by bearing upon My shoulders the Cross whereon I was to hang.

'For the sins of thy hands and arms, with which thou hast done much wickedness, in embrace, touches, and other evil deeds, My hands were driven unto the wood of the Cross by large nails and torn through bearing the weight of My body in Mine agony.

'For the sins of thy heart, with which thou hast sinned through anger, envy, sadness, evil love, and base covetousness, My side and heart were pierced with a sharp spear, and from the wound issued there forth a most potent medicine, sufficient to heal all the passions and sins of the heart—that is to say, water to cool evil desires and loves, and blood for the remission of anger, sadness, and enmity.

' For the sins of thy feet, wherewith thou hast sinned through vain running and dancing and loose walking about for thy pleasure, My feet were not only twisted and bound, but were nailed upon the wood of the Cross ; in place of shoes laced and adorned with cut leather, I had feet all bleeding and covered with the blood which flowed from My whole body.

' But wherefore should I say more ? Howsoever thou mayest discourse, thou canst not find any sin, any disease of the soul, for the which I have not brought the true medicine and given sufficient satisfaction for all sinners and for all the infinite torments and grievous pains which the wretched soul ought to suffer in hell. But if thou remainest not in thy neglectfulness thou needest lament no longer, if only thou doest here suffer with Me and have compassion upon Me always, and be My companion in poverty, ignominy, and contempt as long as thou livest.'

KNOWLEDGE OF GOD AND OF ONESELF

OUR perfection doth certainly consist in knowing God and ourselves ; there is nothing in the whole world whereof I do still delight to write or speak save these two things, namely, the knowledge of God and of ourselves. For this must a man lie ever within the prison of his own self ; and if he obtaineth no profit from this, he must seek another prison.

O, my beloved sons, every vision, every revelation, all sweetness and emotion, all knowledge, all contemplation availeth nothing if man knoweth not God and himself ; for which reason I tell ye truly that without this knowledge all those other things will profit you nothing whatsoever. Wherefore do I marvel that ye desire to have letters from me ; I perceive not in what manner my words can bring you comfort, seeing that I write of naught else save of this knowledge, for I take no more delight in speaking of other things —yea, I have even imposed upon myself silence concerning any other matters. I do beseech you, therefore, that ye pray unto God that He will grant this light unto all generations and that it may remain unto you for ever.

That the knowledge of God is necessary unto us can be proved and made manifest, because that which we strive after is the Kingdom of Heaven. And since we cannot nor ever should strive after it save in the same manner in which the Son of God did attain unto it, it is necessary to know the Son of God and His life and works and those things for the which He did obtain grace, in order that through the imitation of His works and the transforming of ourselves in Him, we may finally follow Him by virtue of His merits and grace,. and with Him possess the Kingdom of Heaven. I say unto you that before all things it is necessary to know Christ, how that He was crucified for us and did suffer the Passion, thereby pointing out unto us the right way of life. For herein hath His infinite charity and His inestimable love been revealed unto us more clearly than in any other of the benefits He hath conferred upon us. For this reason, therefore, and in order that we may not be ungrateful, it is necessary that we should transform ourselves in His love, that is, that we should love Him as He hath loved us, and should love our neighbours ; and likewise that we should lament for the Passion of this our Beloved, seeing how that He was crucified for love of us. Considering, moreover, how many things God hath done for us (and especially for our redemption), we

are required, led, and instructed to reflect upon our
condition ; that is to say, to reflect that our condition
is most noble, being so beloved of the most high God
that He was willing to die for our sake, which He
would not have done if man had not been a most
noble creature and of great worth. We are further
required by this consideration of Christ crucified to
work out our own salvation ; for God Himself, so
exalted (and so far removed and strange unto us),
did use such diligence in obtaining our redemption
and salvation that it is our bounden duty to take heed
for ourselves and our salvation and to further the will
of God, showing penitence for our sins.

The knowledge, therefore, doth afford us infinite
profit in many ways, but chiefly in that we are saved
through His Passion and are filled with His great love.

A constant consideration and a profound knowledge
of Christ crucified are here necessary, for as we behold
so do we love, and the more we do behold of the Son of
God, Jesus Christ the Crucified, the more perfectly
and purely do we love Him and for love do become
one with Him. And according as we do become one
with Him through love, so do we likewise share in the
sufferings which the soul witnesseth in God, the Man
of Sorrows. And seeing that we do love according
as we see and know, so doth the soul lament according
as it beholdeth the sufferings of its Beloved, and doth
suffer with His suffering. Likewise, the more intimately any person knoweth this Man of Sorrows,
the more doth he love Him and suffer with His
sufferings, and through grief is made one with Him
whom he loveth. And as the soul is made one with
this most sweet Christ through love, so is it likewise
united with Him through suffering ; and all this
cometh about through perfect vision and the knowledge of God and of ourselves. In truth, moreover,
since the soul beholdeth the infinitude of the Divine
majesty (of the which I will not speak for fear I should

rather disgrace it than speak of it worthily), and since
it beholdeth, upon the other hand, the vileness and
great unworthiness of sinners (whose friend and kins-
man the most sublime God hath deigned to be, and
for their sake, moreover, hath borne the most shameful
death), it doth sincerely transform itself in the love
of the Son of God, Jesus Christ.

KNOWING GOD IN TRUTH

ABOVE the natural knowledge of God there is a deeper
knowledge which only grace can give.

Before all things it is necessary that he should know
God in very truth, and not only outwardly and
superficially, as though it were through the colour of
writing, or the sound of words, or the likeness of some
creature ; which manner of knowing Him, according
to the common way of speech, is assuredly a simple
knowledge of God.   But man must know Him in very
truth ; he must understand His supreme worthiness,
His supreme beauty, sweetness, exaltedness, virtue,
goodness, liberality, mercy, and pity, and he must
understand that God is the supreme good and highest
of all.   True it is that these things are understood of a
wise person otherwise than of a simple person, for the
wise doth verily understand the matter as it is, whereas
the simple understandeth it only as it doth appear
outwardly.   It is like unto a precious stone which
hath been found and which the wise and the simple
do covet in different ways.   The simple man knoweth
not its virtue and desireth to possess it only for its
beauty and its brightness, and for no other reason ;
but beyond the splendour and the brightness of the
precious stone, the wise man knoweth its virtue and
its worth, and when he hath found it he loveth it
with the utmost intelligence and fervour.   In like
manner doth the wise soul seek to know God, not

only according to the outward appearance and with
only careless reflection, but using all its endeavour
to know Him in very truth, to taste of His supreme
goodness and to know His worth. For not only is
He good, but He is the Supreme Good—and knowing
Him, man doth in all ways love Him for His goodness
—and loving Him, seeketh to possess Him—and He,
who is supremely good, giveth Himself unto the lover,
and the soul feeleth Him and tasteth of His sweetness
and enjoyeth that greatest of all delights. Then doth
the soul participate in that supreme good, the which
is supreme love ; it entereth into it with affection,
and being enamoured of the love of its Beloved, it
desireth to hold Him fast, wherefore it embraceth
Him and presseth Him unto itself ; it uniteth itself
with God and draweth Him unto itself with the utmost
sweetness of love. Then by the virtue of love, is the
lover transformed in the beloved and the beloved is
transformed in the lover, and like unto hard iron
which so assumeth the colour, heat, virtue, and form
of the fire that it almost turneth into fire, so doth the
soul, united with God through perfect grace of Divine
love, itself almost become divine and transformed
in God. Nevertheless, it changeth not its own substance, but its whole life is transformed in the love of
God, and thus doth it almost become divine in itself.

Behold, how greatly it doth profit us to possess a
knowledge of God. And truly is it needful, as hath
been said, that man must know God before he can
walk in His ways and desire to possess Him. There-
after cometh love, which doth transform the lover in
the beloved, and of this nature is the soul who knoweth
God in very truth, and fervently loveth Him whom it
knoweth so well.

Ye must know, however, that the soul cannot
obtain this knowledge of its own power, neither by
writings, nor learning, nor by any created thing—
albeit it may use and profit by them—but solely by

Divine grace and the light thereof. Wherefore do I hold that the soul cannot find it more speedily nor implore it and obtain it more easily from the most high God, perfect Good, perfect Light, and perfect Love, than by devout, pure, constant, humble, and fervent prayer, and that uttered not only with the mouth alone, but with the mind and heart and all the strength of the soul and the feelings of the body, asking and imploring with most ardent desire.

BLESSED JOHN RUYSBROECK

1293–1381

JOHN RUYSBROECK, called 'the Admirable,' was born at
Ruysbroeck, near Brussels, in the year 1293. When he
was eleven he was put in charge of his uncle, John
Hinckaert, a canon of the collegiate church of St. Gudule
at Brussels, who educated him. In 1317, he was ordained
priest and given a chaplaincy at St. Gudule's, but John
found the city very distracting and eventually, in 1343,
together with his uncle, Francis van Coudenberg, and the
holy John of Afflighem, he withdrew to a lonely valley
in the forest of Soignies, called Groenendael ('the green
vale'). Seven years later they all took the habit of the
canons regular of St. Augustine.

At Groenendael, Ruysbroeck gave himself entirely to
contemplation. From time to time he would go into
the forest to write down his reflections ; later on, he was
accompanied by a lay-brother, to whom he dictated. He
became known far and wide ; among his distinguished
visitors were Tauler and Gerard Groot, who was prior of
a neighbouring charterhouse.

Ruysbroeck died in 1381 at the age of eighty-eight,
after a life of the highest contemplation and mystical
union with God. In 1908, his immemorial *cultus* was
confirmed by the Holy See, and his feast is observed by the
Augustinian canons regular.

Blessed John wrote in the Brabant dialect of Flemish,
in order that he might be more widely read and understood. He teaches that the soul can attain Divine union
only by the way of complete renunciation and the dis-
carding of all sensible images. Her most powerful help
comes from the gifts of the Holy Ghost, which enlighten,
cleanse, beautify, and nourish the soul as the sun does
the earth.

Ruysbroeck is unquestionably one of the greatest
contemplatives, and with such as Hadewyck, Sister
Beatrice of Nazareth, and the unknown author of *The
Pearl*, helped Flemish mysticism to reach so high a standard
in the thirteenth and fourteenth centuries.   From the
psychological point of view Ruysbroeck has been bettered,
but from the ontological he is incomparable, a very eagle.
He has been appreciated as much by his successors as by
his contemporaries ;   Denis, the Carthusian, calls him a
' divine teacher,' and Bossuet regarded him as the most
famous and the master of all the mystics of his time.

TRANSLATIONS : *The Sparkling Stone* (London, Dent, 1916).
The Adornment of the Spiritual Marriage (Dent).

The best French translation of Ruysbroeck's writings
is that of the Benedictines of Wisques (Paris, 5 vols.).

WATCH THE BEE

BY means of a comparison Ruysbroeck shows that
we must depend not on the sweetness of Divine
consolation, but on God Himself.

Now I will give you a short similitude, that you
may not err in this case, but may govern yourselves
prudently.   You should watch the wise bee and do
as it does.   It dwells in unity, in the congregation of
its fellows, and goes forth, not in the storm, but in
calm and still weather, in the sunshine, towards all
those flowers in which sweetness may be found.   It
does not rest on any flower, neither on any beauty
nor on any sweetness ;   but it draws from them honey
and wax, that is to say, sweetness and light-giving
matter, and brings both to the unity of the hive,
that therewith it may produce fruits, and be greatly
profitable.

Christ, the Eternal Son, shining into the open
heart, causes that heart to grow and to bloom, and it
overflows with all the inward powers with joy and
sweetness.

So the wise man will do like the bee, and he will

fly forth with attention and with reason and with discretion, towards all those gifts and towards all that sweetness which he has experienced, and towards all the good which God has ever done to him. And in the light of love and with inward observation, he will taste of the multitude of consolations and good things ; and will not rest upon any flower of the gifts of God, but, laden with gratitude and praise, will fly back into the unity, wherein he wishes to rest and to dwell eternally with God.

THE DIVINE SON IN THE VALE OF THE SOUL

Now understand this : when the sun sends its beams and its radiance into a deep valley between two high mountains, and, standing in the zenith, can yet shine upon the bottom and ground of the valley, then three things happen : the valley becomes full of light by reflection from the mountains, and it receives more heat, and becomes more fruitful, than the plain and level country. And so likewise, when a good man takes his stand upon his own littleness, in the most lowly part of himself, and confesses and knows that he has nothing, and is nothing, and can do nothing of himself, neither stand still nor go on, and when he sees how often he fails in virtues and good works : then he confesses his poverty and his helplessness, then he makes a valley of humility. And when he is thus humble, and needy, and knows his own need ; he lays his distress, and complains of it, before the bounty and the mercy of God. And so he marks the sublimity of God and his own lowliness ; and thus he becomes a deep valley. And Christ is a Sun of righteousness and also of mercy, Who stands in the highest part of the firmament, that is, on the right hand of the Father, and from thence He shines into the

bottom of the humble heart ; for Christ is always
moved by helplessness, whenever a man complains
of it and lays it before Him with humility.   Then
there arise two mountains, that is, two desires ; one
to serve God and praise Him with reverence, the
other to. attain noble virtues.   Those two mountains
are higher than the heavens, for these longings touch
God without intermediary, and crave His ungrudging
generosity.   And then that generosity cannot withhold
itself, it must flow forth ; for then the soul is made
ready to receive, and to hold, more gifts.

These are the wherefore, and the way of the new
coming with new virtues.   Then, this valley, the
humble heart, receives three things : it becomes more
radiant and enlightened by grace, it becomes more
ardent in charity, and it becomes more fruitful in
perfect virtues and in good works.

THE INSATIABLE HUNGER FOR GOD

THE more the generous soul glimpses God, the greater
is her hunger and thirst for Him.   This is the grace
which Ruysbroeck describes in the following lines :

Here there begins an eternal hunger, which shall
never more be satisfied ; it is an inward craving and
hankering for the loving power and the created spirit
after an uncreated Good.   And since the spirit longs
for fruition, and is invited and urged thereto by God,
it must always desire its fulfilment.   Behold, now
there begins an eternal craving and continual yearning
in eternal insatiableness.   All such are the poorest
of all men living ; for they are avid and greedy,
and their hunger is insatiable.   Whatever they eat
or drink, they shall never be satisfied, for this hunger
is eternal.   For a created vessel cannot contain an
uncreated Good : and hence there is here an eternal,
hungry craving without satisfaction, and God poured

forth above all and yet staying it not. Here are great
dishes of food and drink, of which no one knows
save he who tastes them : but full satisfaction in fruition
is the dish which is lacking there, and therefore this
hunger is ever renewed. Yet, in the touch, rivers of
honey, full of all delights, flow forth ; for the spirit
tastes these riches in all the ways which it can conceive
and apprehend ; but all this is in a creaturely way and
below God, and hence there remains an eternal hunger
and impatience. Though God gave to such a man all
the gifts which are possessed by all the saints, and
everything that He is able to give, but withheld
Himself, the gaping desire of the spirit would remain
hungry and unsatisfied. The inward stirring and
touching of God makes us hungry and yearning ; for
the Spirit of God hunts our spirit ; and the more it
touches it, the greater our hunger and our craving.
And this is the life of love in its highest working,
above reason and above understanding ; for reason
can here neither give nor take away from love, for our
love is touched by the Divine love.

BURNING AIR AND GLOWING FIRE

In describing the most intimate union with God,
' union without intermediary,' he is careful to avoid
any suggestion of pantheism, as the following passage
shows :

If a man then wishes to penetrate further, with his
active love, into that fruitive love : then, all the
powers of his soul must give way, and they must suffer
and patiently endure that piercing Truth and Goodness which is God's self. For, as the air is penetrated
by the brightness and heat of the sun and iron is
penetrated by fire ; so that it works through fire the
works of fire, since it burns and shines like the fire ;
and so likewise it can be said of the air—for, if the air

had understanding, it could say : ' I enlighten and brighten the whole world '—yet each of these keeps its own nature. For the fire does not become iron, and the iron does not become fire, though their union is without means ; for the iron is within the fire and the fire within the iron ; and so also the air is in the sunshine and the sunshine in the air. So likewise is God in the being of the soul ; and whenever the soul's highest powers are turned inward with active love, they are united with God without means, in a simple knowledge of all truth, and in an essential feeling and tasting of all good.

THE EBB AND FLOW OF GOD

Now understand this : this man shall go out and observe God in His glory with all saints. And he shall behold the rich and generous outflowing of God, with glory and with Himself, and with inconceivable delights towards all the saints, according to the longing of all spirits ; and how these flow back, with themselves, and with all that they have received and can achieve, towards that same rich Oneness from which all bliss comes forth.

This flowing forth of God always demands a flowing back ; for God is a Sea that ebbs and flows, pouring without ceasing into all His beloved according to the need and the merits of each, and ebbing back again with all those who have been thus endowed, both in heaven and on earth, with all that they have and all that they can. And of some He demands more than they are able to bring, for He shows Himself so rich and so generous and so boundlessly good ; and in showing Himself thus He demands love and adoration according to His worth. For God wishes to be loved by us according to the measure of His nobility, and in this all spirits fail ; and therefore their love becomes wayless and without manner, for they know not how they may fulfil it, not how they may come to it. For the love of all spirits is measured : and for this reason their love perpetually begins anew, so that God may be loved according to His demand and to the spirits' own desires. And this is why all blessed spirits perpetually gather themselves together and form a burning flame of love, that they may fulfil this work, and that God may be loved according to His nobility. Reason shows clearly that to creatures this is impossible ; but love always wills the fulfilment of love, or else will be consumed, burned up, annihilated in its own failure. Yet God is never loved according to His worth by any creatures. And to the enlightened reason this is a great delight and satisfaction : that its God and its Beloved is so high and so rich that He transcends all created powers, and can be loved according to His merits by none save Himself.

BLESSED HENRY SUSO

c. 1295–1366

HENRY SUSO belonged to Oberlingen on the lake of Constance, and became a Dominican at an early age. When he was eighteen he dedicated himself to the service of the Eternal Wisdom, and sealed himself thereto by cutting in his flesh the sacred monogram I H S. From 1324 to 1327 he did a post-graduate course of theology at Cologne, where he was a disciple of Eckhart, and wrote his first book, *Büchlein der Wahrheit.* His association with Eckhart brought him under suspicion for a time, and he was removed from his lectorate at Cologne.

In his earlier years Blessed Henry collected a veritable arsenal of 'instruments of penitence,' which he used on himself with excessive zeal. He grew wiser with age, and when he was about forty threw them all into the Rhine, exchanging them for the passive mortifications of the 'dark night of the spirit' and other spiritual and moral trials. He was, for example, accused by one of his penitents of being the father of her child. He gave up his whole being to Christ, keeping his soul peaceful and sweet amid all adversities. 'God is good and He is good to me,' he would reply when asked why he was so cheerful. He died at Ulm in 1366 and was declared blessed in 1831.

Suso collected his spiritual autobiography, his 'Book of Wisdom' and 'Book of Truth,' and a number of letters into one volume called *The Exemplar.* In his writing he is a good literary artist and shows himself a man of sensibility and loving nature. Few books, except the *Imitation,* exceeded his *Eternal Wisdom* in popularity up to the fifteenth century. It sets out how joy flows from suffering, and draws the reader to the realm of contemplation that Suso himself dwelt in so peacefully.

TRANSLATIONS : *Œuvres mystiques du bienheureux Henri*

Suso (2 vols. Paris, 1899). *A Little Book of Eternal Wisdom.* Father C. H. McKenna, O.P. (Burns Oates & 1910).

[handwritten note: Matt 11 28 → Come unto me all who are heavy laden]

GOD'S LOVEABLENESS

Lord, let me reflect on that Divine Thou speakest of Thyself in the book Come over to Me, all ye that desire lled with My fruits. I am the Mother My spirit is sweet above honey and the honeycomb. Wine and music rejoice the heart, but the love of wisdom is above them both.'[1]

Ah, Lord ! Thou canst show Thyself so lovely and so tender, that all hearts must needs languish for Thee and endure, for Thy sake, all the misery of tender desire ; Thy words of love flow so sweetly out of Thy sweet mouth, and so powerfully affect many hearts in their days of youthful bloom, that perishable love is wholly extinguished in them. O my dear Lord, this it is for which my soul sighs, this it is which makes my spirit sad, this it is about which I would gladly hear Thee speak. Now, then, my only elected Comforter, speak one little word to my soul, to Thy poor handmaid ; for, lo ! I am fallen softly asleep beneath Thy shadow, and my heart watcheth.

Eternal Wisdom.—Listen, then, My son, and see, incline to Me thy ears, enter wholly into thy interior, and forget thyself and all things. I am in Myself the incomprehensible good, which always was and always is, which never was and never will be uttered. I may indeed give Myself to men's hearts to be felt by them, but no tongue can truly express Me in words. And yet, when I, the Supernatural, immutable good, present Myself to every creature according to its capacity to be susceptible of Me, I bind the sun's

[1] Ecclesiasticus xxiv, 24, 26, 27 ; xl, 20.

splendour, as it were, in a cloth, and give thee spiritual perceptions of Me and of My sweet love in bodily words thus : I set Myself tenderly before the eyes of thy heart ; now adorn and clothe thou Me in spiritual perceptions and represent Me as delicate and as comely as thy very heart could wish, and bestow on Me all those things that can move the heart to especial love and entire delight of soul. Lo ! all and everything that thou and all men can possibly imagine of form, of elegance, and grace, is in Me far more ravishing than anyone can express, and in words like these do I choose to make Myself known. Now, listen further : I am of high birth, of noble race ; I am the Eternal Word of the Fatherly Heart, in which, according to the love-abounding abyss of My natural Sonship in His sole paternity, I possess a gratefulness before His tender eyes in the sweet and bright-flaming love of the Holy Ghost. I am the throne of delight, I am the crown of salvation, My eyes are so clear, My mouth so tender, My cheeks so radiant and blooming, and all My figure so fair and ravishing, yea, and so delicately formed, that if a man were to lie in a glowing furnace till the day of judgement, only to have one single glance at My beauty, he would not deserve it. See, I am so deliciously adorned in garments of light, I am so exquisitely set off with all the blooming colours of living flowers, that all May-blossoms, all the beautiful shrubs of all dewy fields, all the tender buds of the sunny meads, are but as rough thistles compared to My adornment.

> In the Godhead I play the game of bliss,
> Such joy the angels find in this,
> That unto them a thousand years
> But as one little hour appears.

All the heavenly host follow Me entranced by

new wonders, and behold Me ; their eyes are fixed
on Mine ; their hearts are inclined to Me, their minds
bent on Me without intermission. Happy is he who,
in joyous security, shall take Me by My beautiful hand,
and join in My sweet diversions, and dance for ever
the dance of joy amid the ravishing delights of the
kingdom of heaven ! One little word there spoken by
My sweet mouth will far surpass the singing of all
angels, the music of all harps, the harmony of all
sweet strings. My faithfulness is so made to be loved,
so lovely am I to be embraced, and so tender for pure
languishing souls to kiss, that all hearts ought to break
for My possession. I am condescending and full of
sympathy and always present to the pure soul. I
abide with her in secret, at table, in bed, in the streets,
in the fields. Turn Myself whichever way I will, in
Me there is nothing that can displease, in Me is
everything that can' delight the utmost wishes of thy
heart and desires of the soul. Lo ! I am a good so
pure, that he who in his day only gets one drop
of Me regards all the pleasures and delights of this
world as nothing but bitterness ; all its possessions
and honours as worthless, and only fit to be cast
away ; My beloved ones are encompassed by My
love, and are absorbed into the One Thing alone
without imaged love and without spoken words, and
are taken and infused into that good out of which
they flowed. My love can also relieve regenerate
hearts from the heavy load of sin, and can give a free,
pure, and gentle heart, and create a clean conscience.
Tell Me, what is there in all this world able to outweigh
this one thing ? For he who gives his heart wholly
to Me lives joyfully, dies securely, and obtains the
kingdom of heaven here as well as hereafter.

Now, observe, I have assuredly given thee many
words, and yet My beauty has been as little touched
by them as the firmament by thy little finger, because
no eye has ever seen My beauty, nor ear heard it,

neither has it ever entered any heart. Still let what I have said to thee be as a device to show thee the difference between My sweet love and false, perishable love.

The Servant.—Ah ! Thou tender, delicious, wild flower, Thou delight of the heart in the embracing arms of the pure loving soul, how familiar is all this to him who has even once really felt Thee ; but how strange is it to that man who knows Thee not, whose heart and mind are still of the body ! O, Thou most heart-felt incomprehensible good, this is a precious hour, this is a sweet moment, in which I must open to Thee a secret wound which my heart still bears from Thy sweet love. Lord, plurality in love is like water in the fire. Lord, Thou knowest that real fervent love cannot bear duality. Alas ! Thou only Lord of my heart and soul, my heart desires that Thou shouldst have a particular love for me, and that I should be particularly pleasing to Thy divine eyes. O Lord, Thou hast so many hearts that ardently love Thee, and are of much account with Thee. Alas ! my sweet and tender Lord, how stands it with me in this matter ?

Eternal Wisdom.—My love is of that sort which is not diminished in unity, nor confounded in multiplicity. I am as entirely concerned and occupied with thee alone, with the thought how I may at all times love thee alone, and fulfil everything that appertains to thee, as though I were wholly disengaged from all other things.

The Servant.—O rare ! O wonderful ! whither am I borne, how am I gone astray ! how is my soul utterly dissolved by the sweet friendly words of my beloved ! Oh, turn away Thy bright eyes from me, for they have overcome me.[1] Wherever was there a heart so hard, a soul so lukewarm, so cold as, when it heard Thy sweet living words, so exceedingly fiery

[1] Cant. vi, 5.

as they are, was not fain to melt and kindle in Thy
sweet love ! O wonder of wonders ! that he who
thus sees Thee with the eyes of his soul, should not feel
his very heart dissolve in love ! How right blessed is he
who bears the name of Thy Spouse, and is so ! What
sweet consolations and secret tokens of Thy love
must not he eternally receive from Thee ! O thou
sweet virgin St. Agnes, thou fair wooer of Eternal
Wisdom ! how well couldst thou console thyself
with thy dear Bridegroom, when thou didst say,
' His blood has adorned my cheeks as with roses.'
O gentle Lord, that my soul were but worthy to
be called Thy wooer ! And were it indeed possible
that all delights, all joy and love, that this world
can afford, might be found united in one man, how
gladly would I renounce him for the sake of that name !
How blessed is that man, that ever he was born into
the world, who is named Thy friend, and is so ! Oh,
if a man had even a thousand lives, he ought to stake
them at once for the sake of acquiring Thy love. Oh,
all ye friends of God, all ye heavenly host, and thou
dear virgin St. Agnes, help me to pray to Him ;
for never did I rightly know what His love was.
Alas ! thou heart of mine, lay aside, put away all
sloth, and see if, before thy death, thou mayest
advance so far as to feel His sweet love. O thou
tender beautiful Wisdom ! O my elected one !
What a truly right gracious love Thou canst be above
all loves else in the world ! How very different is Thy
love and the love of creatures ! How false is everything that appears lovely in this world and gives
itself out to be something, as soon as one really begins
to know it. Lord, wherever I might cast my eyes
I always found something to disgust me ; for, if it
was a fair image, it was void of grace ; if it was fair
and lovely, it had not the true way ; or if it had
indeed this, still, I always found something, either
inwardly or outwardly, to which the entire inclination

of my heart was secretly opposed. But Thou art beauty with infinite affability, Thou art grace in shape and form, the word with the way, nobility with virtue, riches with power, interior freedom and exterior brightness, and ONE thing Thou art which I have never found in time, namely, a power and faculty of perfectly satiating every wish and every ardent desire of a truly loving heart. The more one knows Thee, the more one loves Thee ; the more acquainted one is with Thee, the more friendly one finds Thee. Ah me ! what an unfathomable, entirely pure, good Thou art ! See how deceived all those hearts are that fix their affections on anything else ! Ah ! ye false lovers, flee far from me, never come near me more. I have chosen for my heart that one only love in which my heart, my soul, my desire, and all my powers can alone be satiated with a love that never dissolves away. O Lord, could I but trace Thee on my heart ! could I but melt Thee with characters of gold into the innermost core of my heart and soul, so that Thou mightest never be eradicated out of me ! Oh, misery and desolation ! that ever I should have troubled my heart with such things ! What have I gained with all my lovers, but time lost, forfeited words, an empty hand, few good works, and a conscience burdened with infirmity ? Slay me, rather, in Thy love, O Lord, for from Thy feet I will never more be separated.

Eternal Wisdom.—I go forth to meet those who seek Me, and I receive with affectionate joy such as desire My love. All that thou canst ever experience of My sweet love in time, is but as a little drop to the ocean of My love in eternity.

THE WORTH OF TEMPORAL TRIALS

The Servant.—Tell me now, tender Lord, what this suffering is which Thou thinkest so very profitable and good ?

Eternal Wisdom.—What I mean is every kind of suffering, whether willingly accepted or unwillingly incurred—as when a man makes a virtue of necessity in not wishing to be exempt from suffering without My will, and ordering it, in humble patience, to My eternal praise ; and the more willingly he does this, the more precious and agreeable it is to Me. Touching such kinds of suffering, hear further, and write it down in the bottom of thy heart, and keep it as a sign to set before the spiritual eyes of thy soul. My dwelling is in the pure soul as in a paradise of delights, for which reason I cannot endure that she should lovingly and longingly attach herself to anything. But, from her very nature, she is inclined to pernicious lusts, and therefore I encompass her path with thorns. I garnish all her outlets with adversity, whether she like it or not, so that she may not escape from Me ; her ways I strew with tribulation, so that she may not set the foot of her heart's desire anywhere except in the loftiness of My divine nature. And if all hearts were but one heart, they would not be able to bear even that least reward which I certainly will give for the suffering endured by anyone for love of Me. Such is My eternal order in all nature, from which I do not swerve ; what is precious and good must be earned with bitterness ; he who recoils at this, let him recoil ; many are indeed called, but few are chosen.

The Servant.—It may well be, Lord, that suffering is an infinite good, provided it be not without measure, and not too dreadful and overwhelming. Lord, Thou alone knowest all hidden things, and didst create all things in weight, in number and measure; Thou knowest also that my sufferings are measureless, that they are wholly beyond my strength. Lord, is there anyone in all this world who has constantly more painful sufferings than I? They are to me invincible —how am I to endure them? Lord, if Thou wouldst send me ordinary sufferings, I could bear them, but I do not see how I can ever endure such extraordinary sufferings as these—sufferings which in so hidden a manner oppress my heart and soul, which only Thou canst perfectly understand.

Eternal Wisdom.—Every sick man imagines that his own sickness is the worst, and every man in distress, his own distress the greatest. Had I sent thee other sufferings it would have been the same. Conform thyself freely to My will under every pain which I ordain thee to suffer, without excepting this or the other suffering. Dost thou not know that I only desire what is best for thee, even with as kindly a feeling as thou thyself? Hence it is that I am the Eternal Wisdom, and that I know better than thou what is for thy good. Hence it is that thou mayst have felt that the sufferings which I send are much more exquisite, and penetrate deeper, and operate better, for him who does them justice, than all self-chosen sufferings. Why then dost thou so complain to Me? Address Me rather as follows: O my most faithful Father, do to me at all times what Thou wilt!

The Servant.—O Lord, it is so easy to talk, but the reality is so difficult to endure, for it is so very painful.

Eternal Wisdom.—If suffering gave no pain, it could not be called suffering. There is nothing more painful than suffering, and nothing more joyful than to have suffered. Suffering is a short pain and a long joy. Suffering gives to the sufferer pain here and joy hereafter. Suffering kills suffering. Suffering is ordained that the sufferer may not suffer eternally. Hadst thou

so much spiritual sweetness and Divine consolation
and heavenly delight as, at all times, to overflow with
the Divine dew, it would not be for thee so very
meritorious of itself, since, for all this together, I
should not have to thank thee so much ; it could
not exculpate thee so much as an affectionate suffering
or patience in adversity, in which thou sufferest for
My sake.   Sooner will ten be perverted and ruined
in the midst of a great delight and joyous sweetness
than one in the midst of constant suffering and
adversity.   If thou hadst as much science as all the
astronomers, if thou couldst discourse as ably of God
as all the tongues of men and angels, and didst possess
the treasures of knowledge of all the masters, not all
this could avail to advance thee in a good life so much
as if thou didst give thyself up, and didst abandon
thyself in all thy sufferings to God ; for the former
is common to the good and the bad, but the latter
is proper to My elect alone.   If anyone were able
rightly to weigh time and eternity, he ought rather
to desire to lie in a fiery furnace for a hundred years
than to be deprived in eternity of the smallest reward
for the smallest suffering ; for this has an end, but the
other is without end.

The Servant.—Ah, sweet and dear Lord, how like
a sweet harp are these words to a suffering mortal !
Lord, Lord, wouldst Thou but cheer me thus and
come to visit me in my sufferings, I should be glad to
suffer ; it would then be better for me to suffer than
not to suffer.

Eternal Wisdom.—Now, then, hearken to the sweet
music of the distended strings of that Divine harp—
a God-suffering man—how richly it sounds, how
sweetly it vibrates.   Before the world, suffering is a
reproach, but before Me it is an infinite honour.
Suffering is an extinguisher of My wrath, and an
obtainer of My favour.   Suffering makes a man in
My sight worthy of love, for the sufferer is like Me.

Suffering is a hidden treasure which no one can make good ; and though a man might kneel before Me a hundred years to beg a friendly suffering, he nevertheless would not earn it. Suffering changes an earthly man into a heavenly man. Suffering brings with it the estrangement of the world, but confers, instead, My intimate familiarity. It lessens delight and increases grace. He to whom I am to show Myself a friend, must be wholly disclaimed and abandoned by the world. Suffering is the surest way, the nearest way, and the shortest way. He who rightly knows how profitable suffering is, ought to receive it as a gift worthy of God. Oh, how many a man there is who once was a child of eternal death, and plunged in the profoundest sleep, whom suffering has awakened up and encouraged to a good life. How many a wild beast, how many an untamed bird, there is in human form, whom constant suffering has shut up, as it were, in a cage, who, if anyone were to leave him time and place free, would do his best to escape from his salvation. Suffering is a safeguard against grievous falls ; it makes a man know himself, rely on himself, and have faith in his neighbour. Suffering keeps the soul humble and teaches patience. It is the guardian of purity, and confers the crown of eternal salvation. There is probably no man living but who derives good from suffering, whether he be in a state of sin, or on the eve of conversion, or in the fruition of grace, or on the summit of perfection ; for it purges the soul as fire purges iron and purifies gold ; it adorns the wrought jewel. Suffering takes away sin, lessens the fire of purgatory, expels temptation, consumes imperfections, and renovates the spirit. It imparts true confidence, a clear conscience, and constant loftiness of mind. Know that it is a healthy beverage, and a wholesome herb above all the herbs of paradise. It chastises the body which, at any rate, must rot away, but it nourishes

the noble soul which shall endure for ever. Behold,
the noble soul blooms by suffering even as the beautiful
rose by the fresh dews of May! Suffering makes a
wise mind and an experienced man. A man who
has not suffered, what does he know? Suffering is
affection's rod, a paternal blow given to My elect.
Suffering draws and forces men to God, whether they
like it or not. He who is always cheerful in suffering,
has for his servants joy and sorrow, friend and foe.
How often hast thou not thrust an iron bit between
the gnashing teeth of thy enemies, and rendered them,
with thy joyous praise, and thy meekness in suffering,
powerless? Sooner would I create suffering out of
nothing than leave My friends unprovided with it;
for in suffering, every virtue is preserved, man adorned,
his neighbour reformed, and God praised. Patience
in suffering is a living sacrifice, it is a sweet smell of
balsam before My Divine face, it is an appealing
wonder before the entire host of heaven. Never
was a skilful knight in a tournament so gazed at
as a man who suffers well is gazed at by all the heavenly
court. All the saints are on the side of the suffering
man; for, indeed, they have all partaken of it before
him, and they call out to him with one voice that it
contains no poison, but is a wholesome beverage.
Patience in suffering is superior to raising the dead,
or the performing of other miracles. It is a narrow
way which leads direct to the gates of heaven. Suffering
makes us companions of the martyrs, it carries honour
with it, and leads to victory against every foe. Suffering
clothes the soul in garments of rose colour, and in the
brightness of purple; in suffering she wears the
garland of red roses, and carries the sceptre of green
palms. Suffering is for her as a shining ruby in a
young maiden's necklace. Adorned with it, she sings
with a sweet voice and a free heart a new song which
not all the angelic choirs could ever sing, because
they never knew suffering. And, to be short, those

who suffer are called the poor before the world, but before Me they are called the blessed, for they are My elect.

The Servant.—Oh, how plainly does it appear that Thou art the Eternal Wisdom, since Thou canst bring the truth home with such cogency that no one doubts it any longer. No wonder that he, to whom Thou dost make suffering appear so lovely, can bear sufferings. Lord, in consequence of Thy words, all sufferings in future must be easier, and full of joy for me. Lord, my true Father, behold, I kneel before Thee this day, and praise Thee fervently for my present sufferings, and also for the measureless sufferings of the past, which I deemed so very great, because they appeared so hostile to me.

Eternal Wisdom.—But what is thy opinion now?

The Servant.—Lord, my opinion in very truth is this : that when I look at Thee, Thou delight of my eyes, with looks of love, the great and violent sufferings with which, in so paternal a manner, Thou hast disciplined me, and at the sight of which Thy pious friends were filled with such terror on my account, have been like a sweet fall of dew in May.

RICHARD ROLLE

c. 1300–1349

RICHARD ROLLE, the Hermit of Hampole, was born probably at Thornton-le-Dale in Yorkshire ; his parents were poor, but with the help of the archdeacon of Durham, Thomas de Neville, he was able to go to Oxford. It is very probable that he went on to Paris and took his doctorate there, and he may have been a priest : but this is not certain.

When he came back to England he determined to attain his long-cherished wish to be a hermit, and this he did in spite of strong opposition from his father. He reached the heights of contemplation and Divine love, and this same love prompted him to write down his experiences, especially for the benefit of those whom he directed, such as the anchoress Margaret Kirkby of Anderby, and the Cistercia nuns at Hampole. He writes very beautifully, particularly on his favourite subject of God's love. His chief works, e.g. *The Fire of Love* and *The Amending of Life*, were written in Latin, but he also wrote in that mixture of Old English, Norman-French, and Latin, which is the basis of modern English. Rolle has accordingly been called the father of English prose. He was the most prolific of English spiritual writers of the Middle Ages,[1] and many people consider him the greatest. His works were very popular both at home and abroad in mediæval times, and his reputation for holiness brought him visitors from all parts.

WORKS ; *Eight Prose Treatises.* Edited by G. G. Perry. (E.E.T.S., 1921.)

The Fire of Love and the *Mending of Life.* Misyn's translation, edited by R. Harvey. (E.E.T.S., 1896.) Modern translation by F. M. Comper. (London, 1914.)

[1] For an account of them see the excellent book of Dom David Knowles, *The English Mystics* (Burns Oates & Washbourne, 1927).

The Form of Perfect Living. Modernized by Geraldine E. Hodgson. (London, 1910.)
The Minor Works. Edited by the same. (London, 1923.)
The Amending of Life. Edited by A. P. (Burns Oates & Washbourne, 1927.)
Selected Works. Transcribed by G. C. Heseltine. (London, 1930.)

THE THREE DEGREES OF LOVE

MYSTICAL writers have divided love in many ways. Some refer to three degrees, others to four, five, seven, twelve. The division into three degrees by Richard Rolle is a very fine and very original one. It seems to have been specially dear to the author, for he comes back to it in several of his treatises.

Three degrees of love I shall tell thee, for I would that thou might win to the highest. The first degree is called *Insuperable*, the second *Inseparable*, the third *Singular*.

Thy love is *Insuperable* when nothing that is contrary to God's love overcomes it, but it is stalwart against all temptations and stable whether thou be in ease or anguish, in health or sickness. So that thou thinkest that thou wouldst not, for all the world and to have it for ever, at any time make God wrath. And thou wouldst rather, if it should be so, suffer all the pain that might come and all the woe, before thou wouldst do the thing that would displease Him. In this manner shall thy love be *Insuperable*, that nothing may bring it down, but it may be ever springing on high. Blessed is he or she that is in this degree : but they are yet more blessed that might keep this degree and win to the other, that is *Inseparable*.

Thy love is *Inseparable* when all thy heart and thy thought and thy might are so wholly, so entirely and so perfectly fastened, set and established in Jesus Christ, that thy thought goes never from Him, except sleeping : and as soon as thou dost waken, thy heart is on Him saying *Ave Maria* or *Gloria tibi Domine* or *Pater Noster* or *Miserere mei Deus* if thou hast been tempted in thy sleep ; or thinking on His love and His praise as thou didst waking. When thou mayest at no time forget Him, whatsoever thou dost or sayest, then is thy love *Inseparable*. Very great grace have they that are in this degree of love. And I think that thou who hast nothing else to do but to love God, mayest come thereto if any may.

The third degree is highest and most wondrous to win. That is called *Singular*, for it has no peer. Singular love is when all comfort and solace are closed out of thy heart, but that of Jesus Christ alone. It seeks no other joy. For the sweetness of him that is in this degree is so comforting and lasting in His love, so burning and gladdening, that he or she who is in this degree may feel the fire of love burning in their souls as well as thou mayest feel thy finger burn if thou dost put it in the fire. But that fire, though it be hot, is so delectable and wonderful that I cannot describe it.

Then thy soul is Jesus-loving, Jesus-thinking, Jesus-desiring, only breathing in the desire of Him, singing to Him, burning for Him, resting in Him. Then the song of praise and love is come. Then thy thought turns to love and melody. Then it behoves thee to *sing* psalms that before thou didst *say*. Then must thou take long over a few psalms. Then wilt thou think death sweeter than honey, for then thou art full certain to see Him· whom thou lovest. Then mayest thou boldly say : ' I languish for love.' Then mayest thou say : ' I sleep and my heart watches.'

In the first degree men may say : ' I languish for love ' and ' I long for love,' and in the other degree also. For languishing is when men faint because of sickness, and they that are in these two degrees fall from all the desires of this world and from the lust and pleasure of sinful life, setting their intent and their hearts to the love of God. Therefore they may say : ' I languish for love,' and much more they that are in the second degree than in the first. But the soul that is in the third degree is like a burning fire, and as the nightingale that loves song and melody and faints for great love ; so that the soul is so much comforted in the praise and loving of God, and till death comes is singing spiritually to Jesus, and in Jesus, and of Jesus, not crying bodily with the mouth, of which manner of singing I do not speak, for both good and bad have that song, and this manner of song nobody has unless he be in the third degree of love. To which degree it is impossible to come but in great plenitude of love.

Therefore if thou wilt know what kind of joy that song has, I tell thee that no man knows but he or she that feels it, that has it, and that praises God therewith. One thing I tell thee : it is of heaven and God gives it to whom He will, but not without great grace coming before. Who has it thinks all the song and all the minstrelsy of earth but sorrow and woe beside it. In sovereign rest shall they be who may gain it. Wanderers and babblers and those who keep visitors early and late, night and day, or any that are entangled with sin wilfully and wittingly, or that have delight in any earthly thing, they are as far therefrom as heaven is from earth.

In the first degree there are many, in the other degree there are very few, but in the third degree there are scarcely any. For always the greater the perfection is, the fewer followers it has. Men in the first degree may be likened to the stars, in the other to the moon, in the third to the sun. (' The Form of Living.' Chapter VIII.)[1]

[1] *Selected Works of Richard Rolle*, transcribed by G. C. Heseltine. (Longmans, Green & Co., London, 1930), pp. 35–38.

A SONG OF LOVE

My song is a sighing, my life is spent in longing for
the sight of my King, so fair in His brightness.

So fair in Thy beauty! Lead me to Thy light, and
feed me on Thy love! Make me to grow swiftly
in love and be Thou Thyself my prize.

When wilt Thou come, Jesus my joy, to save me from
care and give Thyself to me, that I may see
Thee evermore?

Could I but come to Thee, all my desires were fulfilled.
I seek nothing but Thee alone, who art all my
desire.

Jesus my Saviour! My comforter! Flower of all
beauty! My help and my succour! When
may I see Thee in Thy majesty?

When wilt Thou call me? I languish for Thy presence,
to see Thee above all things. Let not Thy love
for me fail! In my heart I see the canopy that
shall cover us both.

Now I grow pale and wan for love of my beloved
Jesus both God and man. Thy love did teach
me when I ran to Thee, wherefore now I know
how to love Thee.

I sit and sing of the love-longing that is bred in my
breast. Jesus! Jesus! Jesus! Why am I not
led to Thee?

Full well I know Thou seest my state. My thought
is fixed upon love. When I shall see Thee and
dwell with Thee, then shall I be filled and fed.

Jesus, Thy love is constant and Thou knowest best
how to love me. When shall my heart break
forth to come to Thee, my rest?

Jesus, Jesus, Jesus! I mourn for Thee! When may
I turn hence to Thee, my life and my living?

Jesus, my dear and my darling! My delight is to
sing of Thee. Jesus my mirth and my melody!
When wilt Thou come, my king?

Jesus, my salvation and my sweetness, my hope and
my comfort ! Jesus, I desire to die whenever it
shall please Thee. The longing that my Love
has sent to me overwhelms me.

All woe is gone from me, since my breast has been
inflamed with the love of Christ so sweet, whom
I will never leave, but do promise to love always.

For love can cure my evil and bring me to His bliss,
and give me Him for whom I sigh, Jesus, my love,
my sweeting.

A longing has come upon me that binds me day and
night until I shall see His face so fair and bright.

Jesus, my hope, my salvation, my only joy ! Let
not Thy love cool, let me feel Thy love and
dwell with Thee in safety.

Jesus, with Thee alone I am great. I would rather die
than possess all this world and have power over it.

When wilt Thou pity me, Jesus, that I may be with
Thee, to love Thee and look upon Thee ?

Do Thou ordain for me my settle and sit me thereon,
for then we can never part.

And I shall sing of Thy love, in the light of the brightness of Heaven for ever and ever. Amen.

(Transcription by G. C. Heseltine. *Selected Works*,
pp. 98-100.)

A PRAYER TO LOVE

O SWEET and delectable light, that is my infinite
maker, enlighten the face and the vision of my inward
eye with uncreated charity, and kindle my mind
with Thy savour, that, thoroughly cleansed from
uncleanness and made marvellous with Thy gifts, it
may swiftly fly to the high mirth of love ; that I may
sit and rest in Thee, Jesus, rejoicing and going as it
were, ravished with heavenly sweetness ; and that,
established in the beholding of heavenly things, I shall
never be glad but in Divine things.

O Love everlasting, inflame my soul to love God, that nothing may burn in me but His embraces. O good Jesus, who shall grant me to feel Thee, who now neither may be felt nor seen? Shed Thyself into the entrails of my soul! Come into my heart and fill it with Thy most excellent sweetness. Inebriate my mind with the hot wine of Thy sweet love, that, forgetting all evils and all scornful visions and imaginations, and having Thee alone, I may be glad and rejoice in Jesus my God. Henceforward, sweetest Lord, go not from me, but abide with me in Thy sweetness, for Thy presence alone is solace to me and Thine absence alone leaves me sad.

O holy Ghost, that givest grace where Thou wilt, come into me and ravish me to Thyself. The nature that Thou didst make, change with honeysweet gifts, that my soul, filled with Thy delightful joy, may despise and cast away all the things of this world, that it may receive ghostly gifts, given by Thee, and going with joyful songs into infinite light may be all melted in holy love. Burn with Thy fire my reins and my heart that on Thine altar shall burn for ever.

Come, I beseech Thee, O sweet and true Joy! Come, sweet and most desired! Come, my love, who art all my comfort! Come with mellifluous heat into a soul longing for Thee and yearning with sweetest ardour towards Thee. Kindle with Thy heat the whole of my heart, enlightening with Thy light my inmost parts; feed me with the honeysweet song of love, as much as the powers of my body and soul can endure. (' The Amending of Life.' Chapter XI. *Selected Works*, pp. 136–137.)

ON EXCESS OF PENANCE

ONE of the characteristics of Richard Rolle is his great ' reasonableness.' Though himself much addicted to great austerities he repeatedly deprecates the practice of excessive penance.

Some are beguiled with *overmuch abstinence from meat and drink and sleep.* That is a temptation of the devil, to make them fall in the midst of their work, so that they bring it not to an end as they should have done, if they had known reason and kept discretion. And so they lose their merit for their forwardness. This trap our enemy lays to take us with, when we begin to hate wickedness and turn ourselves to God. Then many begin a thing that they may never bring to an end. Then they think they may do whatsoever their heart is set upon. But often they fall ere they reach half-way, and that thing which they thought was for them is hindering them. For we have a long way to heaven, and as many good deeds as we do, as many prayers as we make, and as many good thoughts as we think in truth and hope and charity, so many paces do we go heavenward. Then if we make ourselves so feeble that we may neither work nor pray as we should, nor think, are we not greatly to blame that fail when we have most need to be stalwart? And well I know that it is not God's will that we do so. For the prophet says : 'Lord, I shall keep my strength to Thee.' So that he might sustain God's service to his death-day, and not in a little and in a short time waste it and then lie wailing and groaning by the wall. And the peril is much more than men think. For St. Jerome says that he makes an offering of robbery who excessively torments his body with too little meat or sleep. And St. Bernard says : 'Fasting and watching hinder not ghostly good, but help, if they be done *with discretion*—without that they are vices.' Therefore it is not good to punish ourselves so much and afterwards have no thanks for our deed. ('The Form of Living,' Chapter I, *Selected Works*, p. 17.)

JOHN TAULER

c. 1304–1361

In spite of his great fame we have little certain knowledge of John Tauler. He was born probably at Strasbourg and of a well-to-do family, and he became a Dominican in that city, where he studied philosophy and theology for eight years. There he came under the influence of the current ' Dionysian ' mysticism and of St. Thomas Aquinas, with whom he disagreed on more than one point.

From Strasbourg he seems to have gone to Cologne, where he probably met Blessed Henry Suso and the famous Master Eckhart, whose lectures he may have attended. He was certainly a great admirer of Eckhart, and was the inheritor of his teaching, which he defended from attack, trying to explain in an orthodox sense the propositions condemned by Pope John XXII. Many passages in Tauler's sermons are no more than a faithful echo of Eckhart's thought, but he had the discretion and prudence which his master lacked and carefully modified his over-daring statements ; moreover, he enjoyed mystical experience which would seem to have been denied to Eckhart.

It is believed that Tauler stayed for a time in Paris where he met the masters in theology to whom he so often alludes in his sermons, but in 1336 he was back at Strasbourg. He was then about thirty-two, and already renowned as a zealous apostle and fine preacher. Eighty-three of his authentic sermons are extant, most of them addressed to contemplative Dominican nuns, whose convents were then numerous in the Rhenish provinces. That is probably the reason why he did not consider it necessary to insist over-much on ascetical practices and gave his discourses a very strong mystical appeal. The great sermons in which Tauler explained to the nuns

74

the deep problems which preoccupied him, and of which
he was professor to his Dominican brethren, are of a highly
speculative character ; they deal with the nature of God,
His attributes, the nature and faculties of the soul, the
different ways of attaining to knowledge of God, etc.
Much has been talked about the relations of Tauler
and Ruysbroeck, but little is known about them except
that they probably knew one another at Groenendael.

WORKS : The eighty-three sermons are the only certain
works of Tauler. These have recently been translated
into French by Pères Hugueny and Thery, O.P. (*Editions
de la Vie Spirituelle ;* Paris, 1927). The famous book of
fourteenth-century mysticism called *Erleuchten* is a com-
pilation from the writings of Eckhart, Ruysbroeck, and
Tauler made by St. Peter Canisius (Peter of Nimwegen).[1]
Meditations on the life and Passion of our Lord Jesus Christ.
Attributed to John Tauler. (Burns Oates & Washbourne.)

THE HUNTING OF THE SOUL

IN his sermon for the Monday after Passion Sunday,
Tauler speaks of the Passion and of the soul pursued
by the hounds of temptation.

Summary : How we ought to share the passion of
our Lord. The thirst for God. It increases like the
thirst of a hunted hind. First the big hounds, then the
little ones. A moment's rest and refreshment. The
hind at the water-spring. *Si quis sitit, veniat et bibat*
(John vii, 37).

1. On the last day of the Feast of Tabernacles our
Lord cried aloud, saying, ' If any man thirst, let
him come to Me and drink ! '

We¯ are about to commemorate the worshipful
passion of our Saviour, and no one should part from
the thought of it without his heart being moved to
compassion and gratitude. Since God, our Eternal
Father and our Lord, suffered such shames and pains,

[1] The first book published by a Jesuit.

so those who seek to be His lovers should gladly
suffer with Him : whether good or ill befall them it is
meet that they be joyful in the honour and happiness
that enable them to become like to their friend and to
follow Him in the way He has trodden.

2. He says to us, ' If any man thirst . . .'   What
is this thirst ?   Quite simply, it is this : When the
Holy Spirit comes into the soul and kindles there the
fire of love, the flames throw out blazing sparks
which cause a thirst, a delightsome longing for God ;
sometimes a man does not know what it is that has
happened to account for his distress and his distaste
for all created things.   This longing shows itself in
three ways, according to the three different classes
of people. who experience it : beginners, those who
have made some progress, and those who are called
' perfect,' in so far as perfection is possible in this
world.

3. The holy king David says in his psalter, ' As the
hart panteth after the fountains of water, so my soul
panteth after thee, O God.'   The hart run by hounds
through woods and broken country suffers a thirst
greater than that known to any other animal.   So
the beginner in the ways of charity when temptations
pursue him.   From the moment that he turns from
the world, seven strong hounds are after him : they
are the seven deadly sins, who follow him with temptations far stronger than he has known before ; formerly
they took him by surprise, now he is conscious of them
all the time, according to the word of Solomon :
' Son, when thou comest to the service of God . . .
prepare thy soul for temptation.'   The hotter this
chase becomes the greater is the thirst and the more
burning the desire for God.   Sometimes it happens
that a hound comes up with its quarry and hangs
on to the hart's belly with its teeth ; when it can't
shake it off, the hart drags the dog to a tree and crushes
its head against it until it looses hold. . . . A man

has to do an exactly similar thing. When he has not the mastery over pursuing temptations he must hasten to the tree of the Cross and Passion of our Lord Jesus Christ, banging temptation's head against it until it is broken ; there man can triumph and be free.

4. But when the hart has shaken off the hounds he is often pestered by terriers snapping around him, and though he keeps them away with horns and hoofs they eventually tire him out. So again with man. Having got the victory over big sins, he does not guard sufficiently against occasions of smaller faults : chance acquaintances, wordly company, fine clothes, innocent recreations, such trifles can take a bite here and a bite there, that is to say, they can dissipate a man's heart and conscience until, like the hart, his religious life gets weakened. His enthusiasm and devotion are lost, every thought of God and Divine things may vanish, and thus the terriers can do him more harm than serious temptations : against them he is on his guard, but for the little things he is not careful. It is the same with all things whose danger we don't realize or about which, while harmless in themselves, we are insufficiently careful : they may be much more harmful than those whose danger we know.

And just as the hunted stag gets hotter and more thirsty so indeed does the Divine heat and thirst increase in man as each temptation thrusts him towards God, where alone he can find truth and peace, justice and pity.

5. When the hart is worn out and failing, the huntsmen sometimes call off the hounds (when they are sure they won't lose their animal) and give it a few minutes' ' breather ' so that it may run the better. Our Lord does in like manner. When He sees that the stress of temptation is being too much for a man, He gives him relief therefrom and touches his lips with a sweet taste of Divine things. Man is so

strengthened thereby that he feels himself rise above all his wretchedness, and everything that is not God seems nothing worth—but it is only refreshment for further pursuit : at the moment when he least expects it the hounds are at his throat more fiercely than ever and he has need of all his fresh courage and strength.

God's tenderness and love for us are the cause of this pursuit, for thus man, the hunted stag, runs towards the God who is his true goal ; thus is he made greatly to long and thirst after Him who is all truth, all peace, and the fullest consolation ; thus is the drink that will satisfy that thirst made yet more desirable and delightful both here in time and later in eternity. Then, man will drink open-throatedly at the source of the sweetest of all water-springs, the heart of the Father ; now, he experiences such consolation that all things earthly seem worthless, and suffering for God's sake is as nothing.

6. When the hart has eluded the hounds and reached water he gives himself up to quenching his thirst at his ease. Man, when with Divine help he has shaken off the rabble of dogs, big and little, and reached God, does the same : he drinks at the sacred fountain till he is filled and intoxicated with God, and in the fullness of his happiness forgets himself completely. Then does it seem to him that he could work miracles, pass through fire and water and massed swords, face death itself ; he fears neither life nor death, pleasure nor pain. In this state of exultation some-times he weeps, sometimes sings, sometimes laughs.

Then the rationalists come along. They know nothing of the marvellous works which the Holy Spirit can do in His own, for they can recognize nothing beyond the gifts of nature. And they say, ' Good Lord ! How worked up and excited you are ! ' . . . But the lovers of God pass into a wordless peace, where all is happiness and joy ; whatever happens to them, whatever they do, that joy and peace remain, the flames of love leap within them, and the heat makes their heart boil over with happiness. (Sermon for the Monday before Palm Sunday, t. I, pp. 257–262, in *Sermons de Tauler*, traduction par les RR.PP. Hugueny et Théry. Paris, 1927.)

ABANDONMENT TO THE DIVINE WILL

In his three Epiphany sermons he teaches us to rise above ourselves by renouncing our own will, thus preparing the soul for God's work.

Summary : What God wishes above all. The Divine call : *Surge !* One response : by personal effort. The other response : by docile submission to God's will. The wonderful results of this. Difference between the two states of soul. What the submissive soul must do. *Surge et illuminare, Hierusalem* (Is., lx, 1).

1. God wants only one thing in the whole world, the thing which it needs, but He wants it so strongly that the whole of His care is given to it. That thing is to find the innermost part of the noble spirit of man clean and ready for Him to accomplish the Divine purpose therein. God has all power in Heaven and on earth ; but the power to do the finest of His works, in man, against man's will He has not got.

2. What then must man do so that God's light and doing may shine in his inmost part ? He must raise himself ; *Surge*, says the text : ' Arise ! ' Man has to help in the Divine work by lifting himself above self, above creatures, above all that is not God, and by so doing there is born in us an ardent wish to abstract ourselves from and take away from ourselves all unlikeness to Him. The more a man succeeds in this, the more the desire grows, the higher he gets above self, and often, when the inmost soul is stripped,

and touched, the desire gets into his very flesh and
bones.

3. Two different sorts of people answer to this
interior touch in two different ways.

The one meets it with his own natural ability and
disturbs his soul with rational concepts and high
speculation ; he silences the wish by wanting to listen
to and understand these big thoughts. Such an one
finds in them a great satisfaction and imagines that
he is a Jerusalem and that he has found peace in the
activity of his own reasoning powers. Or else he seeks
satisfaction in self-chosen observances, devotions,
meditations, whether of his own invention or imitated
from others. He proposes to prepare his soul by these
means, finds peace in them, and supposes himself to
have become a Jerusalem. But he finds this peace
only in those devotional observances and works that he
has himself selected and arranged, and in no others.

That this is a false peace may easily be recognized
from the fact that those who act thus still display
their own personal faults, pride, self-indulgence, bodily
solicitude, spitefulness, judging of their fellows. If
somebody upsets them they complain at once of
injuries done to them on purpose and out of dislike.
They seem willingly to consent to many of their own
shortcomings. Clearly they have got ready their own
souls for their own purposes ; God cannot work in
them : and therefore their peace is a delusion. They
have not really arisen. They ought not to deceive
themselves with the idea that they are a Jerusalem
and that they have found true peace all by themselves ;
they should strive more seriously to overcome their
weaknesses and to follow our Lord Jesus Christ in
humility and charity, dying to themselves in all things
and so learning to raise themselves up.

4. The other category consists of those noble souls
who really ' arise,' and thereby are enlightened.
They leave their interior spiritual preparation to God

and put themselves completely in His hands. They put everything from them and keep nothing for themselves, neither in good works nor ' devotions,' in what they do or what they don't do, neither here nor there, in gladness or in sorrow ; they receive all from God in humble fear and at the same time give all back to Him in an entire despoiling and resolute abandonment of self to the Divine will. With that they are always satisfied, in weal and in woe, for that, the good and acceptable will of God, is the one thing they regard and value.

To these people may be applied the words of Jesus to His disciples when they urged Him to go into Judæa for the Feast of Tabernacles : ' Go you up to this festival day, your time is always ready. But I go not up, because My time is not accomplished.' Their time is all the time, to give themselves up to God at every moment ; but His time, to do and to enlighten, is at His own disposition and will, and must be awaited with patient submission.

5. The radical distinction between these people and those mentioned before is that they leave the preparing of their inmost soul to God and do not try to do it themselves. Nor do they escape the criticism of the others (nobody does), but if they be convicted of sin, whether pride or sensuality or worldliness or unjust anger or hate or any other wickedness, they at once return humbly to God and again put themselves at the disposition of His will. They in truth arise, for they put self beneath their feet and become a true Jerusalem, finding peace amid strife, and gladness amid misery. They accept God's will, and therefore the whole world cannot wrest their peace from them : devils and men in league cannot deprive them of it. They savour God and nought else, and are truly enlightened, for He pours out His pure light upon them at every turn, even, nay, particularly, at the times when their darkness seems most thick.

These men are supernatural men, Divine men, and God is in their every action ; indeed, if I may put it so, they, in a sense, *are* no longer, but God is in them. They are the most loveable of men ; they bear up the world, they are its columns and piers. Great is the happiness of him who can keep himself in that state.

6. The people who want to prepare their own souls and not give themselves up to God have their faculties entangled in their faults to such a degree that they cannot free them. They don't even want to, but prefer the pleasure of following their own wills.

But the others, who have risen above themselves to God, hasten to Him with their misfortune at the first onslaught and victory of sin, in such a way that there is no longer sin, because they enjoy a godlike freedom.

7. Ought not these people, while God prepares their inmost spirit, to undertake on their side some external works ? Should they not be up and doing ? Not necessarily.[1] The text says *Surge*, and that in itself is a work ; moreover, their own particular work which they must be always at, without a break, as long as they live, without which no man can attain perfection. They must be all the time raising themselves, keeping their hearts towards God, freeing the deeps of their soul, asking themselves humbly and fearfully, ' Where is He who is born ? ' and watching out for what God wants that they may do it. If He wishes them to be passive, passive they will be ; if active, then active ; or if contemplative, then will they rejoice in contemplation. They know interiorly that it is God who has made ready the inner room of their soul, and He wishes to dwell therein to the exclusion of all His creatures.

God works within the first class of men *by inter-*

---

[1] Tauler does not repudiate exterior works, penances, religious exercises ; but he sees them valuable only to the degree that they are required by the Holy Ghost.

mediary, in the second class *without intermediary*.[1] But what He does in these noble and holy souls in immediate contact with Him no one can explain ; one man cannot tell such things to another ; only he can know who has experienced it, and if it indeed be God who has entered into possession of his soul he can say nothing of it. While external works completely disappear for these men, the interior consciousness of God increases, and when one reaches the highest point of which his grace-aided diligence is capable he continues in a state of entire self-nothingness, according to the words of Christ : ' When you shall have done all these things that are commanded you, say, We are unprofitable servants.' Man is never so perfect that he can leave his humble fear, and at the highest degree of perfection he must needs always say and think, *Fiat voluntas tua :* ' Lord, may Thy will be done ! ' And he has to watch with careful attention to see that there is not the smallest inordinate attachment to no matter what, lest God should find something in his soul to hinder the accomplishment of the Divine purpose without intermediary.

May we be enabled thus to arise, that God may do His work in us, and may the all-loving Lord help us so to do ! Amen. (Third sermon for the Epiphany. *Op. cit.* t. I, pp. 197–204.)

TRUE PRAYER

' BE sober and watch ! Because your adversary, the Devil, as a roaring lion goeth about seeking whom he may devour ' (I Pet., v, 8). Watch, that is to say, be

---

[1] We are in the presence of God without intermediary when we are conscious of His life in us directly, without the help of any created image. This exalted way of prayer is a special gift of God and it cannot be obtained by effort of our personal meditations, even with the help of the Faith and habitual graces ordinary to the Christian life.

vigilant in prayer.   Now what sort of prayer had St.
Peter in mind ?   Not prayer of words (which some
people, for instance, those who say over numberless
psalms, call prayer exclusively), but that which our
Lord meant when He said that true worshippers
worship in spirit and in truth.   The saints and teachers
of the Church tell us that prayer is a lifting-up of the
mind to God.   Reading and vocal prayer help in
this lifting-up, and it is good to use them for this
purpose ; just as my clothes are useful to me, but
are not me, so spoken words are a help to true prayer
without being that prayer : its essence is that the heart
and mind go out to God without intermediary.   True
prayer is simply that, and nothing else : the lifting-up
of the mind to God in love, interior longing for and
humble submission to Him.

Clergy are bound to the recitation of the Divine
Office, but no prayer is so full of love and worship as
the sacred Our Father which our sovereign master
Christ Himself taught to us, and it conduces to true
essential prayer better than any other.   It is a heavenly
prayer, which the blessed sing and meditate upon
without ceasing.

St. Augustine says that there is a mysterious place
deep in the soul that is beyond time and this world,
a part higher than that which gives life and movement
to the body ; true prayer so raises the heart that God
can come into this innermost place, the most disinterested, intimate, and noble part of our being, the
seat of our unity.   It is His eternal dwelling-place,
and into this grand and mysterious kingdom He
pours the sweet delight of which I have spoken.   Then
is man no longer troubled by anything : he is recollected, quiet, and really himself, and becomes daily
more detached, spiritualized, and contemplative, for
God is within him, reigning and working in the
depths of his soul.   This spiritual state of man cannot
be compared with what has gone before, for he has

now taken on a Divine life ; the spirit is set in God, drowned in that fire of charity which is essentially and of its nature God Himself.

Those so happy as to reach this state turn anew to their duties as Christians and direct their prayers and desires to God to ask Him for all things which He wants them to ask ; they remember their friends, sinners, the souls in Purgatory, they seek in their love to satisfy the needs of every man in Christendom, not by praying individually for Joan or for Mrs. Brown,[1] but in a simplified and essential way. Just as with a single look I can see you all here, sitting in front of me, so can they, in the manner of contemplatives, see the whole world. Then they again turn their eyes inward to the burning depths of Divine love and rest therein, and its flames drop like dew upon all the needy in Christendom, returning again to their Divine source.

Thus do these souls go out and return and yet remain in the delightsome and silent deeps where they live and move and have their being. Wherever and whenever we meet them we find that their life is as it were Divine ; all their sayings and doings are godlike. These noble people serve for the good of the whole of Christendom : in them man is aided and consoled, in them God is glorified ; they live in Him, and He lives in them. We are bound to reverence them, always and everywhere.

May we all, God helping us, reach to these heights ! Amen. (Extract from the sermon in preparation for Whitsuntide. *Op. cit.*, t. II, pp. 22–24.)

---

[1] The original has ' for dame Matilda or for Kunegondis ' (Tr.).

THE AUTHOR OF
'THE CLOUD OF UNKNOWING'
Fourteenth century

THE name even is not known of the author of *The Cloud of Unknowing* and other similar treatises, such as *The Epistle of Privy Counsel*, but he certainly lived during the fourteenth century. He is generally thought to belong to its second half, after Richard Rolle and before Walter Hilton. He is far less celebrated than Rolle, but it is none the less true that he may be regarded as the most delicately acute and original of the English mystical writers. The understanding of him is not always easy, especially for a beginner.

Both the 'Cloud' and the other treatises are full of the ideas of the pseudo-Dionysius, who is often mentioned. Its basic idea, explaining the title, is that God is so far above our knowledge as to be hidden in a cloud of unknowability. It is only by emptying the mind of all created images and the will of all temporal affections that we can arrive at the supreme earthly knowledge of God, a knowledge that consists in knowing that we know nothing about Him and that He infinitely transcends all our apprehensions of Him, however subtle and exalted they may seem.[1]

WORKS : *The Cloud of Unknowing and Other Treatises.* Edited by Dom Justin McCann (Burns Oates & Washbourne, 1924). An excellent edition, including *The Epistle of Privy Counsel*, the translation of the mystical theology of Dionysius, and a commentary on the ' Cloud,' by Father Augustine Baker, O.S.B.

---

[1] No writer sets forth the same doctrine so well and so similarly to the Englishman as the disciple of St. John of the Cross, Father de Quiroga, O.C.D. His treatise on contemplation was written in Spanish and has not yet been translated into English or French.

CONTEMPLATION

CONTEMPLATION, according to the author, consists in the union of the soul with God through the aspirations of a loving heart called ' meek stirrings of love,' aspirations made in the cloud of unknowing with a confused, very simple and imageless knowledge of God, who is apprehended as the unknowable. Father Baker, in his commentary of *The Cloud of Unknowing*, identifies that contemplation with his own ' prayer of aspirations ' and the confused knowledge of faith of which he often speaks.

HOW THE WORK OF THIS BOOK (CONTEMPLATION) SHALL BE WROUGHT AND OF THE WORTHINESS OF IT BEFORE ALL OTHER WORKS.

Lift up thine heart unto God with a meek stirring of love ; and mean Himself and none of His goods. And thereto look that thou loathe to think on aught but Himself, so that nought work in thy mind nor in thy will but only Himself. And to do that in thee is to forget all the creatures that ever God made and the works of them so that thy thought or thy desire be not directed or stretched to any of them, neither in general nor in special. But let them be, with a seemly recklessness (heedlessness), and take no heed of them.

This is the work of the soul that most pleases God. All saints and angels have joy of this work and hasten them to help it with all their might. All fiends be mad when thou dost so, and try for to defeat it in all that they can. All men living on earth be wonderfully helped by this work, thou knowest not how. Yea, the souls in purgatory are eased of their pains by virtue of this work. Thou thyself art cleansed and made virtuous by no work so much. And yet it is the lightest work of all, when a soul is helped with grace in a sensible list (delight) and soonest done. But else it is hard and wonderful for thee to do.

Cease not therefore, but travail therein till thou feel list. For at the first time when thou dost it, thou findest but a darkness, and as it were a *cloud of unknowing*, thou knowest not what, saving that thou feelest in thy will a naked intent unto God. This darkness and this cloud, howsoever thou dost, is betwixt thee and thy God, and hindereth thee, so that thou mayest not see Him clearly by light of understanding in thy reason, nor feel Him in sweetness of love in thine affection. And therefore shape thee to bide in this darkness as long as thou mayest, evermore crying after Him whom thou lovest. For if ever thou shalt see Him or feel Him, as it may be here, it must always be in this cloud and in this darkness. And if thou wilt busily travail as I bid thee, I trust in His mercy that thou shalt come thereto. (*The Cloud of Unknowing*, Chapter 3.)[1]

HOW TO ATTAIN GOD BY A NEGATIVE KNOWLEDGE

THAT RIGHT AS BY THE FAILING OF OUR BODILY WIT WE BEGIN MOST READILY TO COME TO THE KNOWING OF GHOSTLY THINGS SO BY THE FAILING OF OUR GHOSTLY WITS WE BEGIN MOST READILY TO COME TO THE KNOWLEDGE OF GOD, SUCH AS IS POSSIBLE BY GRACE TO BE HAD HERE.

And therefore travail fast in this nought, and in this nowhere, and leave thine outward bodily wits

---

[1] *The Cloud of Unknowing and Other Treatises* with a commentary on the 'Cloud' by Fr. Augustine Baker, O.S.B., edited by Dom Justin McCann. Orchard Books, No. 4 (Burns Oates & Washbourne, 1924), pp. 11–13.

(senses) and all that they work in : for I tell thee truly that this work may not be conceived by them.

For by thine eyes thou mayest not conceive of anything, unless it be by the length and by the breadth, the smallness and the greatness, the roundness and the squareness, the farness and the nearness, and the colour of it. And by thine ears, nought but noise or some manner of sound. By the nose, nought but either stench or savour. And by thy taste, nought but either sour or sweet, salt or fresh, bitter or pleasant. And by the feeling, nought but either hot or cold, hard or tender, soft or sharp. And truly neither has God nor ghostly things none of these qualities nor quantities. And therefore leave thine outward wits, and work not with them, neither within nor without : for all those that set them to be ghostly workers within, and ween that they should either hear, smell, see, taste, or feel ghostly things, either within them or without, surely they are deceived and work wrong against the course of nature.

For by nature they be ordained that with them men should have knowing of all outward bodily things and in no wise by them come to the knowing of ghostly things. I mean by their works. By their failings we may, as thus : when we hear speak or read of certain things, and also conceive that our outward wits cannot tell us by any quality what those things be, then we may be verily certified that those things be ghostly things, and not bodily things.

In this same manner ghostly it fareth within in our ghostly wits when we travail about the knowing of God Himself. For have a man never so much ghostly understanding in knowing of all made ghostly things, yet may he never by the work of his understanding come to the knowing of an unmade ghostly thing : the which is nought but God. But by the failing he may. Because that thing that he faileth in is nothing else but only God. And therefore it was that St. Denis said : ' *the most godly knowing of God is that which is known by unknowing.*' And truly whoso will look in Denis' books, he shall find that his words will clearly confirm all that I have said or shall say, from the beginning of this treatise till the end. (*The Cloud of Unknowing*, Chapter 70.)

THE PRAYERS OF A CONTEMPLATIVE

IN the following passage the author shows how simple and highly spiritual the prayers of a real contemplative should be.

And right as the meditations of them that continually work in this grace and this work (of contemplation) rise suddenly without any means (without any reading or special considerations), right so do their prayers. I mean their special prayers, not those prayers that be ordained by the Holy Church. For they that be true workers in this work, they worship no prayer so much as those of Holy Church ; and therefore they do them, in the form and in the statute that they be ordained by holy fathers before us. But their special prayers rise evermore suddenly unto God, without any means or any premeditation, in special coming before, or going therewith.

And if they be in words, as they be but seldom, then be they in full few words : yea, and the fewer the better. Yea, and if it be but a little word of one syllable, methinks it is better than of two, and more according to the work of the spirit ; since a ghostly worker in this work should evermore be in the highest and the sovereignest point of the spirit. That this be truth see by ensample in the course of nature. A man or a woman, affrighted by any sudden chance of fire, or of a man's death, or whatever else it may be, suddenly in the height of his spirit he is driven in haste and in need to cry or to pray for help. Yea, how ?

Surely not in many words, nor yet in one word of
two syllables. And why is that? Because he thinks
it over long tarrying, for to declare the need and the
work of his spirit. And therefore he bursteth up
hideously with a great spirit, and crieth but one
little word of one syllable : such as is this word FIRE
or this word OUT. (Alas !).

And right as this little word FIRE stirreth rather
and pierceth more hastily the ears of his hearers,
so doth a little word of one syllable, when it is not
only spoken or thought, but secretly meant in the
depth of the spirit ; the which is the height : for in
ghostliness all is one, height and depth, length and
breadth. And rather it pierceth the ears of Almighty
God than doth any long psalter unmindfully mumbled
in the teeth. And therefore it is written that short
prayer pierceth heaven. (*The Cloud of Unknowing.*
Chapter 37, pp. 91-93.)

SUPREME DETACHMENT OF THE
TRUE CONTEMPLATIVE

THAT ALL KNOWING AND FEELING OF A MAN'S OWN
BEING MUST NEEDS BE LOST IF THE PERFECTION OF
THIS WORK SHALL VERILY BE FELT IN ANY SOUL IN
THIS LIFE.

Look that naught work in thy mind nor in thy
will but only God. And try to smite down all knowing
and feeling of aught under God, and tread all down
full far under the *cloud of forgetting.* And thou shalt
understand that in this work thou shalt forget not only
all other creatures than thyself, or their deeds or thine,
but also thou shalt in this work forget both thyself
and thy deeds for God, as well as all other creatures
and their deeds. For it is the condition of a perfect
lover, not only to love that thing that he loveth,

more than himself; but also in a manner to hate himself for that thing that he loveth.

Thus shalt thou do with thyself: thou shalt loathe and be weary with all that thing that worketh in thy mind and in thy will, unless it be only God. For otherwise surely, whatsoever it be, it is betwixt thee and thy God. And no wonder if thou loathe and hate to think of thyself, when thou shalt always feel sin a foul stinking lump, thou knowest never what, betwixt thee and thy God: the which lump is none other than thyself. For thou shalt think it oned and congealed with the substance of thy being: Yea, as it were without separation.

And therefore break down all knowing and feeling of all manner of creatures, but most busily of thyself. For on the knowing and feeling of thyself hangeth the knowing and the feeling of all other creatures; for in regard of it, all other creatures be lightly forgotten. For if thou wilt busily set thee to the proof, thou shalt find, when thou hast forgotten all other creatures and all their works—yea, and also all thine own works—that there shall remain yet after, betwixt thee and thy God, a naked knowing and a feeling of thine own being: the which knowing and feeling must always be destroyed, ere the time be that thou mayest feel verily the perfection of this work. (*The Cloud of Unknowing*, Chapter 43, pp. 103-105.)

JULIAN OF NORWICH

1342–c. 1415

ALL that is known about Dame Julian is what she tells us herself in her book of ' revelations,' with the addition of a few details (such as her name and domicile) which we owe to the early copiers of the manuscript. She was probably a Benedictine nun before she went to live as a recluse in a cell adjoining St. Julian's Church at Norwich, where the window may still be seen whereat she assisted at Mass.

She says in her revelations that she wished to have an illness and to have ' bodily sight ' of our Lord's sufferings, that she might the better share in them. Her wish was granted, and on May 8, 1373, when she was 'thirty and one-half years of age,' the crucified Christ appeared to her and ' revelations ' followed one another for more than a day without interruption, in the form of bodily and imaginative visions, supernatural speech, and intellectual visions—a happening probably unique in hagiology. Julian reflected on these things for twenty years, receiving more light and complementary revelations on their meaning and significance. She seems at first to have written a short account of them (which is extant), and later, at least twenty years after the principal visions, she set down the definitive results of her long contemplation in the book of the *Revelations of Divine Love*.

These revelations can be divided into two classes. The first is the bodily and imaginative visions, showing Jesus on the Cross to the end that Dame Julian should have a livelier understanding of His pains, as she had desired. But these visions are different from those of St. Catherine de Ricci, Anne Catherine Emmerich, and other ecstatics, in that they were, so to say, points of departure for our Lord's teachings and not representations of His passion at which the visionary is merely present.

The other class of vision is intellectual, concerned ordinarily with some point of theology, and making one think in some ways of the ' Dialogues ' of St. Catherine of Siena. It was principally these that were the subject of Dame Julian's later meditations and they are the most interesting part of her book. She questions our Lord on such matters as the problem of evil, the existence of sin, predestination, an endless hell, and comments on them. She shows herself to be a deep-rooted ' optimist,' largely on account of our Lord's revelation to her of the immensity of His love. She learned from it that that love is the key to all our agonizing problems, for it is the origin and cause of all that is. Thenceforward the Redemption, the existence of evil, the possibility of sin, all such things were seen in the blazing light of Divine love and nought could trouble her, for ' all is made a bliss by love.'

Julian of Norwich is undoubtedly the most charming of English mystical writers, and perhaps the greatest. Her book stands beside those of Angela of Foligno, Catherine of Siena, and Teresa of Avila.

WORKS : *XVI Revelations of Divine Love.* Edited by Dom Serenus Cressy. First edition 1670, latest edition 1902.

The same. Modern edition edited by Dom Roger Hudleston (Burns Oates & Washbourne, 1927).

The Shewings of Lady Julian. The first version of the revelations, edited by the Rev. Dundas Harford. (London, 1925.)

JESUS OUR MOTHER

BUT now behoveth to say a little more of this forth-spreading, as I understand in the meaning of our Lord : how that we be brought again by the Mother-hood of Mercy and Grace into our Nature's place,[1] where that we were made by the Motherhood of kind Love : which Kindly-love it never leaveth us.

Our Kind Mother, our Gracious Mother,[2] for that

---

[1] MS. ' kyndly-stede.'
[2] i.e., our Mother by Nature, our Mother in Grace.

He would all wholly become our Mother in all things,
He took the ground of His Works full low and full
mildly in the Maiden's womb. (And that He showed
in the First [Showing] where He brought that meek
Maid afore the eye of mine understanding in the
simple stature as she was when she conceived.) That
is to say : our high God is sovereign Wisdom of all :
in this low place He arrayed and dight Him full
ready in our poor flesh, Himself to do the service and
the office of Motherhood in all things.

The Mother's service is nearest, readiest, and surest :
[nearest, for it is most of nature ; readiest, for it is
most of love ; and surest[1]] for it is most of truth.
This office none might, nor could, nor ever should do
to the full, but He alone. We wit that all our mother's
bearing is [bearing of] us to pain and to dying :
and what is this but that our Very Mother, Jesus, He
—All-Love—beareth us to joy and to endless living ?—
blessed may He be ! Thus He sustaineth us within
Himself in love ; and travailed, unto the full time
that He would suffer the sharpest throes and the
grievous-est pains that ever were or ever shall be ;
and died at the last. And when He had [so] done,
and so borne us to bliss, yet might not all this make
full content[2] to His marvellous love ; and that showeth
He in these high overpassing words of love : ' If I
might suffer more, I would suffer more.'

He might no more die, but He would not stint of
working : wherefore then it behoveth Him to feed
us ; for the dearworthy love of Motherhood hath
made Him debtor to us. The mother may give her
child suck [of] her milk, but our precious Mother,
Jesus, He may feed us with Himself, and doeth it,
full courteously and full tenderly, with the Blessed
Sacrament that is precious food of very life ; and with all
the sweet Sacraments He sustaineth us full mercifully

---

[1] These clauses, omitted from the MS., are in Cressy's version.
[2] MS. ' makyn asseth.'

and graciously. And so meant He in this blessed word where that He said : ' I it am that Holy Church preacheth thee and teacheth thee.' That is to say : ' All the health and life of Sacraments, all the virtue and grace of My Word, all the Goodness that is ordained in Holy Church for thee, I it am.' The Mother may lay the child tenderly to her breast, but our tender Mother, Jesus, He may homely lead us into His blessed breast, by His sweet open side, and show therein part of the Godhead and the joys of Heaven, with ghostly sureness of endless bliss. And that showed He in the Tenth [Showing], giving the same understanding in this sweet word where He saith : ' Lo ! how I loved thee'; beholding into His side, rejoicing.

This fair lovely word *Mother*, it is so sweet and so kind itself[1] that it may not verily be said of none but of Him ; and to her that is very Mother of Him and of all. To the property of Motherhood belongeth kind love, wisdom, and knowing ; and it is good : for though it be so that our bodily forthbringing be but little, low, and simple in regard of our ghostly forthbringing, yet it is He that doeth it in the creatures by whom that it is done. The Kind, loving Mother that witteth and knoweth the need of her child, she keepeth it full tenderly, as the kind and condition of Motherhood will. And as it waxeth in age, she changeth her working, but not her love. And when it is waxen of more age, she suffereth that it be beaten[2] in breaking down of vices, to make the child receive virtues and graces. This working, with all that be fair and good, our Lord doeth it in them by whom it is done : thus He is our Mother in kind by the working of Grace in the lower part for love of the higher part. And He willeth that we know this : for He will have all our love fastened to Him. And in this I saw that all our duty that we owe, by God's

---

[1] MS. ' so kynd of the self.'   [2] MS. ' brinstinid.'

bidding, to Fatherhood and Motherhood, for [reason of] God's Fatherhood and Motherhood is fulfilled in true loving of God ; which blessed love Christ worketh in us. And this was showed in all [the Revelations] and especially in the high plenteous words where He saith : ' It is I that thou lovest.'

THE USE OF FAULTS

AND after this He suffereth some of us to fall more hard and more grievously than ever we did afore, as us thinketh. And then ween we (who be not all wise) that all were naught that we have begun. But it is not so. For it needeth us to fall, and it needeth us to see it. For if we never fell, we should not know how feeble and how wretched we are of our self, and also we should not fully know that marvellous love of our Maker. For we shall see verily in heaven, without end, that we have grievously sinned in this life, and notwithstanding this, we shall see that we were never hurt in His love, nor were never the less of price in His sight. And by the assay of this falling we shall have an high, marvellous knowing of love in God, without end. For hard and marvellous is that love which may not, nor will not, be broken for trespass. And this is one understanding of profit. Another is the lowness and meekness that we shall get by the sight of our falling : for thereby we shall highly be raised in heaven ; to which raising we might[1] never have come without that meekness. And therefore it needeth us to see it ; and if we see it not, though we fell it should not profit us. And commonly, first we fall and later[2] we see it : and both of the Mercy of God.

The mother may suffer the child to fall sometimes, and be dis-eased in diverse manners for its own profit, but she may never suffer that any manner of peril

---

[1] i.e., could.   [2] MS. ' syth.'

come to the child, for love. And though our earthly
mother may suffer her child to perish, our heavenly
Mother, Jesus, may not suffer us that are His children
to perish : for He is All-Mighty, All-wisdom, and All-
love ; and so is none but He—blessed may He be !

But oftentimes when our falling and our wretchedness is showed us, we are so sore adread, and so greatly
ashamed of our self, that scarcely we wit where we
may hold us. But then willeth not our courteous
Mother that we flee away, for Him were nothing
lother. But He willeth then that we use the condition
of a child : for when it is dis-eased, or adread, it
runneth hastily to the mother for help, with all its
might. So willeth He that we do, as a meek child
saying thus : ' My kind Mother, my Gracious Mother,
my dearworthy Mother, have mercy on me : I have
made myself foul and unlike to thee, and I nor may
nor can amend it but with thy privy help and grace.'
And if we feel us not then eased forthwith, be we sure
that He useth the condition of a wise mother. For if
He see that it be more profit to us to mourn and to
weep, He suffereth it, with ruth and pity, unto the
best time, for love. And He willeth then that we use
the property of a child, that evermore kindly trusteth
to the love of the mother in weal and in woe.

JESUS CRUCIFIED

AND in this dying was brought to my mind the words
of Christ : ' *I thirst.*'

For I saw in Christ a double thirst : one bodily ;
another ghostly, the which I shall speak of in the
Thirty-first Chapter.

For this word was showed for the bodily thirst :
the which I understood was caused by failing of
moisture. For the blessed flesh and bones was left all
alone without blood and moisture. The blessed body

dried alone long time, with wringing of the nails and
weight of the body. For I understood that, for
tenderness of the sweet hands and of the sweet feet,
by the greatness, hardness, and grievousness of the
nails the wounds waxed wide and the body sagged,
for weight by long time hanging. And [therewith
was] piercing and wringing of the head, and binding
of the Crown all baked with dry blood, with the sweet
hair clinging, and the dry flesh, to the thorns, and the
thorns to the flesh drying ; and in the beginning
while the flesh was fresh and bleeding, the continual
sitting of the thorns made the wounds wide. And
furthermore I saw that the sweet skin and the tender
flesh, with the hair and the blood, was all raised and
loosed about from the bone, with the thorns where-
through it were digged in many pieces, as a cloth
that were sagging, as if it would hastily have fallen
off, for heaviness and looseness, while it had natural[1]
moisture. And that was great sorrow and dread to
me : for methought I would not for my life have
seen it fall. How it was done I saw not ; but understood it was with the sharp thorns and the boisterous
and grievous setting on of the Garland [of Thorns]
unsparingly and without pity. This continued awhile,
and soon it began to change, and I beheld and
marvelled how it might be. And then I saw it was
because it began to dry, and stint a part of the weight,
and set about the Garland. And thus it environed
all about, as it were garland upon garland. The
Garland of the Thorns was dyed with the blood, and
the other garland [of Blood] and the head, all was one
colour, as clotted blood when it is dry. The skin of
the flesh that showed of the face and of the body, was
small-wrinkled with a tanned colour, like a dry board
when it is skinned ;[2] and the face more brown than
the body.

I saw four manner of dryings : the first was bloodless ;

---

[1] MS. ' kind.'   [2] i.e., when the bark is stripped off.

the second was pain following after ; the third, hanging up in the air, as men hang a cloth to dry ; the fourth, that the bodily kind asked liquor and there was no manner of comfort ministered to Him in all His woe and dis-ease. Ah ! hard and grievous was His pain, but much more hard and grievous it was when the moisture failed and all began to dry thus clinging.

These were the pains that showed in the blessed head : the first wrought to the dying, while it was moist ; and that other, slow, with clinging drying, with blowing of the wind from without, that dried and pained Him with cold more than mine heart can think.

And other pains—for which pains I saw that all is too little that I can say : for it may not be told.

The which Showing of Christ's pains filled me full of pain. For I wist well He suffered but once, but [this was as if] He would show it me and fill me with mind as I had afore desired. And in all this time of Christ's pains I felt no pain but for Christ's pains. Then thought-me : ' I knew but little what pain it was that I asked ' ; and, as a wretch, repented me, thinking : ' If I had wist what it had been, loth me had been to have prayed it.' For methought it passed bodily death, my pains.

I thought : ' Is any pain like this ? ' And I was answered in my reason : ' Hell is another pain : for there is despair. But of all pains that lead to salvation this is the most pain, to see thy Love suffer. How might any pain be more to me than to see Him that is all my life, all my bliss, and all my joy, suffer ? ' Here felt I soothfastly[1] that I loved Christ so much above myself that there was no pain that might be suffered like to that sorrow that I had to see Him in pain.

[1] i.e., in truth.

THE SOUL'S TRUE REST

IN this same time our Lord showed me a ghostly sight
of His homely loving.

I saw that He is to us everything that is good and
comfortable for us. He is our clothing that for love
wrappeth us, claspeth[1] us, and all becloseth us for
tender love, that He may never leave us ; being to us
all-thing that is good, as to mine understanding.

Also in this He showed [me] a little thing, the
quantity of an hazel-nut, in the palm of my hand ;
and it was as round as a ball. I looked thereupon
with eye of my understanding, and thought : ' What
may this be ? ' And it was generally answered thus :
' It is all that is made.' I marvelled how it might
last, for methought it might suddenly have fallen to
naught for little[ness]. And I was answered in my
understanding : ' It lasteth, and ever shall [last] for
that God loveth it.' And so all thing hath the Being
by the love of God.

In this Little Thing I saw three properties. The
first is that God made it : the second is that God
loveth it : the third, that God keepeth it. But what
is to me soothly the Maker, the Keeper, and the
Lover,—I cannot tell ; for till I am substantially
oned[2] to Him, I may never have full rest nor very
bliss : that is to say, till I be so fastened to Him,
that there is right naught that is made betwixt my
God and me.

It needeth us to have knowing of the littleness of
creatures and to naughten[3] all thing that is made, for
to love and have God that is unmade. For this is the
cause why we be not all in ease of heart and soul :
that we seek here rest in those things that be so little,
wherein is no rest, and know not our God that is

---

[1] MS. ' halfyth us.'   [2] i.e., united.
[3] i.e., to make naught of.

Almighty, All-wise, All-good. For He is the Very
Rest. God will[eth to] be known, and it liketh Him
that we rest in Him ; for all that is beneath Him
sufficeth not us. And this is the cause why that no
soul is rested till it is naughted of[1] all things that
are made. When it is wilfully naughted, for love to
have Him that is all, then is it able to receive ghostly
rest.

Also our Lord God showed that it is full great
pleasance to Him that a silly soul come to Him
nakedly and plainly and homely. For this is the
kind yearnings of the soul, by the touching of the
Holy Ghost (as by the understanding that I have in
this Showing). ' God, of Thy Goodness, give me
Thyself : for Thou art enough to me, and I may
nothing ask that is less, that may be full worship to
Thee ; and if I ask anything that is less, ever me
wanteth—but only in Thee I have all.'

And these words are full lovesome to the soul, and
full near touch they the will of God and His Goodness.
For His Goodness comprehendeth all His creatures
and all His blessed works, and overpasseth[2] without
end. For He is the endlessness, and He hath made us
only to Himself, and restored us by His blessed
Passion, and keepeth us in His blessed love ; and all
this is of His Goodness.

ST. CATHERINE OF SIENA

1347–1380

CATHERINE was the youngest but one of the twenty-five children of a dyer, Graciomo di Benincasa. From very early childhood she was a visionary and practised austerities, and later on resolutely refused to think of marriage, to the annoyance of her parents. She lived as a recluse in her father's house for a time, at the age of sixteen became a secular Dominican tertiary, and later rejoined her family. She had already experienced many visions and other mystical experiences, consolatory and frightening, and in 1366 was spiritually wedded to our Lord, who told her to undertake a life of active apostolate. She began by attempting to calm the civil strife of her native city, counselling the magistrates and party leaders and looking after the captives and casualties.

Catherine's influence became enormous and she was known through Italy. A 'spiritual family' gathered round her : men and women of all ranks, clerics and lay people, who called her 'mother' and alternately helped and bothered her. In 1375 she received the *stigmata*, but invisibly at her own prayer, and in the following year she went to Pope Gregory XI at Avignon and succeeded—where so many had failed—in persuading him to return to Rome. His successor, Urban VI, summoned Catherine to Rome as his counsellor, in 1378, and there she died two years later, offering her life for the peace of the Church that was already being torn by the 'great schism.'

TRANSLATIONS: *The Dialogue of the Seraphic Virgin St. Catherine of Siena.* Translated by Algar Thorold (The Newman Press, 1950).

Life of St. Catherine of Siena. By Alice Curtayne. (London, 1931.)

THE ATTAINMENT OF PERFECT LOVE

Catherine : I know, Lord, that Your will and my perfecting are to be sought in the sovereign love of Yourself, so I want to fulfil this righteousness and to love You with this sovereign love as ardently as I may. But how must I set about it ? I do not understand that sufficiently and I beseech You to enlighten me more.

Our Lord : Listen attentively with your whole mind. To love Me perfectly three things are necessary.

In the first place : To purify and direct the will in its temporal loves and bodily attachments so that nothing passing and perishable is loved except because of Me. The important thing is not to love Me for your own sake, or yourself for your own sake, or your neighbour for your own sake, but to love Me for Myself, yourself for Myself, your neighbour for Myself. Divine love cannot suffer to share with any earthly love, and you lack in perfection and transgress My love in the measure that you let temporal things detract from it. In order to be disinterested and holy the soul should be averse from what is pleasing to the body. Behave in such a way that the created things I have given to you as a means to warm and increase your love should do so, and not have the contrary effect of hindering it. I have made and given them to you that you should learn a better idea of My limitless goodness therefrom and so love Me yet more. Pull yourself together, then ! Gird up your loins, control your senses, be careful, master the unruliness of the desires which the conditions of mortal life and the defect of human nature raise on every side, so that you may be able to say with the prophet, ' O thou who hast formed my feet '—that is, my affections, which are the feet of the soul, ' like those of the deer '—to run from the hounds, the dangerous deceits of inordinate desires, 'Thou shalt set me in an high place'—namely, contemplation.

In the second place : When you have reached the first stage, you will be able to go on to the second, which needs a greater perfection. Take My honour and My glory as the sole end of your thoughts, your actions, and all that you do ; try always to worship Me, whether it be by prayer, by words, or by deeds ; do all you can to help your neighbour to have the same state of mind, so that everyone you meet may know, love, and worship Me like you and with you. This doing will be yet more pleasing to Me, for by it My purpose will be more advanced.

In the third place : If you do that which I am going to tell you now, you will have reached a consummate perfection and nothing will be wanting in you. It is the attainment of an ardently desired and perseveringly sought disposition of the soul in which you are so closely united with Me and your will so conformed to My perfect will that you never wish not only evil, but even the good that I do not wish ; in every circumstance of this wretched life, whether spiritual or temporal interests are involved, whatever the difficulties, you possess your soul in peace and quietness, having always an unshakeable faith in Me, your Almighty God, knowing that I can love you more than you can love yourself and that I watch over you a thousand times more carefully than you can watch over yourself. The more trustfully you give yourself up to Me, the more I shall be watching over you ; you will gain a clearer knowledge of Me and experience My love more and more delightfully.

Such perfection can be reached only by a steady, continuous, and absolute renunciation of self-will. To refuse this renunciation is to refuse true perfection. He who renounces willingly by the same act does My will perfectly ; his life is pleasing to Me and I am with him, for I love above all to dwell in mankind

and work in them by grace—' My delight is to be with
the children of men.' I must not infringe the rights
of your freedom ; but I will transform you in Myself,
since you wish it, and make you one with Me by
making you share in My perfection, particularly in
My tranquillity and My peace. (*Dialogue sur la Perfection*, tr. par R. P. Bernadot, O.P.)

DIVINE PROVIDENCE

How blind they are who do not see that everything
which God allows to happen is ordained for our
good and our salvation.

' I want to make you see, My well-beloved daughter,
what patience I have to exercise in sustaining the
creatures which I have made most lovingly (as I have
told you) in My own image and likeness. Open the
eyes of your understanding and look at Me. . . .'

Thereupon this soul turned the eyes of her mind,
enlightened by the light of our most holy Faith, and
fixed them upon the Divine Majesty with burning
desire, for the words she had heard had taught her
better to understand the truth of God's good providence.
Obeying His word, she looked into the abyss of charity,
and there saw how He was the sovereign and eternal
Goodness, how for love He created and then redeemed
us by the blood of His Son, and how this same love
was the source of all His many gifts to us, whether
sufferings or joys. All comes from love, and all God
does is ordered toward the salvation of mankind.
That is the truth that she saw in the Blood poured
out with such a lavishness of love.

Then the eternal and all-governing Father said to
her :

' Those who are indignant at and rebel against the
things that befall them are blind with self-love. I
speak to you now in general and in particular, and

I say that they take for evil and regard as misfortunes, ruin, evidence of hate towards themselves, the things that I do out of love and for their good, that they may be saved from eternal loss and receive the life which shall not pass away. Why then do they murmur against Me? Because they have put their trust in themselves, and so all becomes dark for them and they do not know things as they are : wherefore they hate what they should reverence and in their pride would judge My secret judgements which are righteousness itself. They are like blind men who try by touch or by taste or by hearing to appraise the worth of things that cannot be estimated by those senses alone. They will not turn to Me, the true light, Who feeds their souls and their bodies, without Whom they are not. When somebody does something for them it is I who have prompted the deed and given that creature the ability and knowledge and will to do them that service. These foolish people want to rely only on what they can feel with their hands. But touch is deceptive : it lacks light, whereby colour may be discerned ; nor can taste alone be trusted, for it does not see the noxious germ upon the food ; the ear can be misled by a sweet sound, because it does not see the singer, and trusting in the voice alone you may come upon death.

' So it is with these blind folk who have lost the light of reason fulfilled by faith : they will believe only the evidence of their senses, like him who tests a thing with his hands alone. The pleasures of the world seem lovely to them : but as they do not really see them they do not take into account that these pleasures are like a piece of good cloth that is full of thorns, that much grief and many cares wait upon them, and that the heart that cherishes them without reference to Me cannot bear the burden of itself. These pleasures seem to have a good taste to the mouth, that is, to an inordinate desire for them, but they are alive with foul microbes, a swarm of deadly sins that infect the soul, deprive her of the life of grace, and so disfigure her that she loses her likeness to Me.

'They listen to the voice of self-love, and think what a nice sound they hear. And why? Because the soul, left to herself, makes a bee-line for self-indulgence and is all ears for the song that betrays her; she troubles about nothing else, but follows the entrancing voice that leads to ruin; then she falls into the ditch, the nets of sin entangle her, and she is in the hands of her enemies. I was no longer anything to her, I, her guide and her path; she was blinded with self-love, with confidence in her own powers and her own knowledge. The path has been shown to her by My Son, the Word, when He said, "I am the way, the truth, and the life." Whoever walks in it cannot lose his way or be overtaken by darkness, nor can any come to Me except through Him, for He and I are one. I have already told you that I have made of My Son a bridge over which all may come to their proper end, but for all that men will not trust Me, although I am concerned only for their sanctification. My great love ordains or permits everything that happens to that end alone—and they are always shocked at me. I bear with them patiently and protect them, for I love them even though they do not love Me—and they unrelentingly return Me revolt, hate, complaints, endless unfaithfulness. They do not even know themselves, and yet in their blindness they want to see the most secret purposes that I ordain in justice and love. But he who does not know himself cannot truly know Me or understand My judgements; and all things else he sees distortedly.' (*Le dialogue de Ste. Catherine*, tr. par R. P. Hurtaud, O.P., Paris, 1931, t. II, pp. 160–164.)

THE STATE OF PERFECT SOULS

Such ones thirst after suffering and are ceaselessly conscious of the Divine presence.

'Now I have told thee how it is to be seen that souls have arrived at the perfection of love, friendly and filial. Now I do not want to conceal from thee how great is the delight with which they taste Me, though they are still in the mortal body. This is because, having arrived at the third state, they acquire the fourth, which, however, is not separated from the third, but is united with it, and the one cannot be without the other, except in the same way as love of Me can be without love of the neighbour. A fruit that arises from this third condition of the soul's perfect union with Me, wherein she acquires fortitude, is that not only does she bear with patience, but she anxiously desires to suffer pain for the glory and praise of My name. Such as these glory in the shame of My only-begotten Son, as said Paul, my standard-bearer : *" I glory in tribulations, and in the shame of Christ crucified "* —and in another place—*" God forbid that I should glory save in Christ crucified "*—and again—*" I bear in my body the stigmata of Christ crucified."* Such as these, I say, as if enamoured of My honour, and famished for the food of souls, run to the table of the most Holy Cross, willing to suffer pain and endure much of the service of the neighbour, and desiring to persevere and acquire the virtues, bearing in their body the stigmata of Christ crucified, causing the crucified love which is theirs to shine, being visible through self-content and delighted endurance of the shames and vexations on every side. To these, My most dear sons, trouble is a pleasure, and pleasure and every consolation that the world would offer them are a toil, and not only the consolation that the servants of the world, by My dispensation, are constrained to give

them, in reverence and in compassion of their corporal
necessities, but also the mental consolation which
they receive from Me, the eternal Father. Even this
they despise through humility and self-hatred. They
do not despise consolation itself, which is My gift
and grace, but only the pleasure which the soul's
appetite finds therein. And this they do through the
virtue of true humility, obtained through holy self-
hatred, which is the nurse and nourisher of love,
and has been acquainted through true knowledge of
themselves and of Me. Wherefore, as thou seest,
the virtues and wounds of Christ crucified shine in
their bodies and souls. Such as these do not feel any
separation from Me, as happens in the case of others,
of whom I have told you, namely, that I would leave
them, not by grace, but by feeling, afterwards returning
to them again. I do not act thus to these most perfect
ones who have arrived at the great perfection, and
are entirely dead to their own wills, but I remain
continually both by grace and feeling in their soul,
so that at any time that they wish they can unite their
mind to Me, through love. They can in no way be
separated from My love, for, by love, they have
arrived at so close a union. Every place is to them an
oratory, every moment a time for prayer—their
conversation has ascended from earth to heaven—
that is to say, they have cut off from themselves every
form of earthly affection and sensual self-love, and
have risen alone themselves into the very height of
Heaven, having climbed the staircase of virtues and
mounted the three steps which I figured to thee,
in the body of My Son.'

ECSTATIC UNION

GOD often tempers the vehemence of His union with
the chosen soul, without withdrawing consciousness
of His presence.

' I have said that, from these perfect ones, I never withdraw by sentiment. But in another way I depart from them, for the soul, being bound in the body, is not sufficient continually to receive that union which I make with her, and because she is not sufficient, I withdraw Myself, not by sentiment or by grace, but by that union which I make with her. For souls, arising with anxious desire, run, with virtue, by the capital bridge of the doctrine of Christ crucified, and arrive at the gate, lifting up their minds in Me, and in the blood, and burning with the fire of love they taste in Me, the eternal Deity, Who am to them a sea pacific, with Whom the souls have made so great union, and she has no movement except in Me. And, being yet mortal, they taste the good of the immortals, and having yet the weight of the body, they receive the joy of the spirit. Wherefore oftentimes, through the perfect union which the soul has made with Me, she is raised from the earth almost as if the heavy body became light. But this does not mean that the heaviness of the body is taken away, but that the union of the soul with Me is more perfect than the union of the body with the soul ; wherefore the strength of the spirit, united with Me, raises the weight of the body from the earth, leaving it as if immovable and all pulled to pieces in the affection of the soul. Thou rememberest to have heard it said of some creatures, that were it not for My goodness, in seeking strength for them, they would not be able to live, and I would tell thee, that, in the fact that the souls of some do not leave their bodies is to be seen a greater miracle than in the fact that some have arisen from the dead, so great is the union which they have with me. I, therefore, sometimes for a space withdraw from the union, making the soul return to the vessel of her body, that is, to the sentiment of the body, from which she was separated through the affection of love. From the body she did not depart, because that cannot be, except in death ; the bodily powers alone departed, becoming united to Me through affections of love. The memory is full of nothing but Me ; the intellect, elevated, gazes upon the object of My Truth ; the affection, which follows the intellect, loves and becomes united with that which the intellect sees. These powers, being united and gathered together and immersed and inflamed in Me, the body loses its feeling, so that the seeing eye sees not, and the hearing ear hears not, and the tongue does not speak, except as the abundance of the heart will sometimes permit it for the alleviation of the heart and the praise and glory of My name.

'The hand does not touch and the feet walk not because the members are bound with the sentiment of love, and, as it were, contrary to all their natural functions, cry to Me, the Eternal Father, for the separation of the soul from the Body, as did My glorious Paul, saying : " *O·wretched man that I am, who will separate me from this body ? for I feel within me a perverse law which wars against the Spirit.*" Paul was not referring to the warring of senses against the Spirit, from which he knew he was secured by My words : *My grace is sufficient for thee.* Why then did he utter those words for Me ? Because he found himself bound in the vessel of the body, which for a space of time impeded his vision of Me. That is to say, until death, his eyes were bound so as not to be able to see Me, the Eternal Trinity, who am in the sight of the blessed immortals, who render praise and glory to My name. Whereas he found himself in the midst of mortals who always offend Me, deprived of the sight of Me, that is, of Me in My essence.'

WALTER HILTON

d. 1396

LITTLE enough is known of the life of Walter Hilton. For a long time he was supposed to have been a Carthusian monk, but he was in fact an Austin canon regular at Thurgarton in Nottinghamshire, where he died on March 24, 1396. He was a great friend of the Carthusians, who in turn admired him, and his writings, which within a hundred years of his death were known throughout England, France, and neighbouring countries, were passed on from charterhouse to charterhouse.

His principal work is *The Ladder of Perfection*, which was printed by Wynkyn de Worde in 1494, a systematic treatise written for a nun who was probably an anchoress. It covers the whole spiritual life, showing what is required in preparation for the life of union with God in contemplation, of which a masterly analysis is presented. The *Ladder* may be called, in a figure of speech that is continually suggested by it, a ' guide-book ' for the journey to the spiritual Jerusalem, namely, the ' contemplation in perfect love of God.'

Hilton wrote two other treatises of less importance, which were both printed early in the sixteenth century. One, *To a Devout Man in Temporal Estate*, contains spiritual counsels for a layman of high rank ; the other, *The Song of Angels*, is more specifically mystical and describes the heavenly delights enjoyed by the purified soul. Other treatises are attributed to Hilton, most of which are still unpublished, and his reputation was so great in England during the fifteenth century that he was accepted as the author of the *Imitation of Christ*. His style of writing has not the attractiveness of that of the author of *The Cloud of Unknowing* or of Dame Julian and lacks the poetical imagery and warmth of Rolle ; on the other hand, he is clear and methodical, displaying theological profundity and a wide knowledge of the Bible, St. Augustine, St. Gregory, St. Bernard, and above all of St. Thomas and the scholastics. Hilton was more widely known and appreciated than his predecessors, and his *Ladder of Perfection* in particular was a powerful influence during the fifteenth century, especially in the formation of religions.

WORKS : *The Scale of Perfection.* With an introduction by Dom M. Noetinger (Burns Oates & Washbourne, 1927).
The Minor Works of Walter Hilton. Edited by Dorothy Jones (Burns Oates & Washbourne, 1931).

THE PARABLE OF A DEVOUT PILGRIM

THE most famous passage of *The Ladder of Perfection* is surely the one in which Hilton, under the parable of a pilgrim going to Jerusalem, describes the various difficulties which a devout soul has to overcome before reaching the city of peace, viz. the blessed state of union with God in loving contemplation. Father Baker did not hesitate to reproduce the whole passage (three chapters) somewhat paraphrased in his *Sancta Sophia.* We give here the second and third chapter.

Now thou art in the way, and wottest how thou shalt go. Now beware of enemies that will be busy to let thee if they may. For their intent is to put out of thine heart that desire and the longing thou hast to the love of Jesus, and to drive thee home again to the love of worldly vanities, for there is nothing that grieves them so much. These enemies are principally fleshly desires and vain dreads, that rise out of thy heart through corruption of thy fleshly kind, and would let they desire of the love of God, that they might

fully and restfully occupy thine heart; these are thy
next enemies. Also other enemies there be, as unclean
spirits that are busy with sleights and wiles to deceive
thee. But one remedy shalt thou have that I said
before; whatsoever it be that they say, trow them
not, but hold forth thy way and only desire the
love of Jesus. Answer ever thus: I am naught, I
have naught, I covet naught, but only the love of
Jesus.

If thine enemies say to thee first thus, by stirrings
in heart, that thou art not shriven aright, or that there
is some old sin hid in thy heart that thou knowest not,
nor never were shriven aright, and therefore thou must
turn home again and leave thy desire (of going to
Jerusalem) and go shrive thee better: trow not this
saying for it is false, for thou art shriven. Trust
securely that thou art in the way, and needest no more
ransacking of shrift for that which is past. Hold
forth thy way and think on Jerusalem.

Also if they say that thou art not worthy to have the
love of God, whereto shalt thou covet that thou might
not have, nor art not worthy thereto; trow them
not, but go forth and say thus: ' Not because I am
worthy, but because I am unworthy, therefore
would I love God; for if I had it, that would
make me worthy. And since I was made thereto,
though I should never have it, yet will I covet it,
and therefore will I pray and think that I might
get it.'

And then if thine enemies see that thou beginnest
to wax bold and well willed to thy work, they begin
to wax afraid of thee. Nevertheless they will not
cease from tarrying thee whenever they may, as long
as thou art going on the way, what with dread and
menacing on the one side, what with flattering and
false pleasing on the other side, to make thee break
thy purpose and turn home again. They will say
thus: If thou hold forth thy desire to Jesus so fully

travailing as thou beginnest, thou shalt fall into sickness or into fantasies, or into frenzies, as thou seest that some do ; or thou shalt fall into poverty and bodily mischief ; and no man shall well help thee. Or thou might fall into privy temptations of the fiend, that thou shalt not help thyself. For it is wonderful perilous to any man to give him fully to the love of God, and leave all the world, and covet nothing, but only the love of Him ; for so many perils may befall that a man knoweth not of. And therefore turn home again and leave this desire, for thou shalt never bring it to the end ; and do as other worldly men do.

Thus say thine enemies, but trow them not, but hold forth thy desire and say naught else, but thou wouldest have Jesus, and be at Jerusalem. And if they perceive then thy will so strong that thou wilt not spare neither for sin nor for sickness, for fantasies nor for frenzies, for doubts nor for dreads of ghostly temptations, for mischief nor for poverty, for life nor for death ; but ever forth thou wilt one thing and nothing but one, and makest deaf ear to them as though thou heard them not, and holdest thee forth stiffly in thy prayer and in thy other ghostly works without stinting, with discretion after the counsel of thy sovereign (superior) or of thy ghostly father, then begin they to be wroth and go a little nearer thee. Then they begin to rob thee and beat thee, and do thee all the shame they can. And that is when they bring it to pass that all the deeds that thou dost, be they never so well done, are deemed of other men as ill and turned into the worst part. And whatsoever it be that thou wouldest have done in help of thy body or of thy soul, it shall be letted or hindered by other men ; so that thou shalt be put from thy will in all things that thou skilfully covetest. And all this they do that thou shouldest be stirred to ire or melancholy or evil will against thy even-Christian. But against all these dis-eases, and all other that thou mayest feel, use this remedy. Take Jesus in thy mind, and anger thee not with them, tarry not with them, but think on thy lesson, that thou art naught, that thou hast naught, that thou mayest naught lose of earthly good, thou covetest naught but the love of Jesus, and hold forth thy way to Jerusalem with thy occupation.

And nevertheless if thou be tarried sometime through frailty of thyself with such uneases as fall to thy bodily life, through evil will of man or malice of the fiend, as soon as thou mayest come again to thyself, leave off the thinking of thy dis-ease and go forth to thy work. Abide not too long with them for dread of thine enemies.

And after this, when thine enemies see that thou art so well willed . . . then they are much abashed. But then will they assay thee with flattering and vain pleasing. And that is when they bring to the sight of thy soul all thy good deeds and virtues, and bear upon thee that all men praise thee and speak good of thy holiness, and how all men love thee and worship thee for thy holy living. Thus do thine enemies that thou shouldst think their saying sooth, and have delight in this vain joy and rest thee therein. But if thou do well, thou shalt hold all such jangling as falsehood and flattery of thine enemy, that proffereth thee to drink venom tempered with honey, and therefore refuse it and say thou wilt not thereof, but thou wouldest be at Jerusalem.

Such lettings thou shalt feel or else other like unto them, what of thy flesh, what of the world, what of the fiend more than I can rehearse now. For a man as long as he suffereth his thought wilfully to run about the world in beholding of sundry things, he perceiveth few lettings, but as soon as he draws all his thought and his yearning to one thing only, to have that, to know that, to love that, and that is only Jesus, then shall he feel many painful lettings, for

everything that he feels which is not that that he covets
is letting to him.

Therefore I have told thee of some specially, as
for example ; and overmore I say generally that what
stirring that thou feelest of thy flesh or of the fiend,
pleasant or painful, bitter or sweet, liking or dreadful,
gladsome or sorrowful, that would draw down thy
thought and thy desire from the love of Jesus, to
worldly vanity, and would let utterly thy ghostly
covetousness that thou hast to the love of Him, and
that thy heart should be occupied with that stirring
restingly, set it at naught, receive it not wilfully, tarry
not therewith too long.

But if it be of some worldly thing that behoveth
needs to be done to thyself or to thine even-Christian,
speed thee soon of it and bring it to an end, that
it hang not on thy heart. If it be another thing that
needeth not, or else that toucheth thee not, charge it
not, jangle not therewith, nor anger thee not, dread
it not, like it not, but smite it out of thine heart readily,
and say thus : ' I am naught, I have naught, naught
I seek nor covet, but the love of Jesus.'

Knit thy thought to this desire, and strengthen it
and maintain it with prayer and with other ghostly
works that thou forget it not, and it shall lead thee in
the right way and save thee from all perils, and though
thou feel them, thou shalt not perish, and I hope that
it shall bring thee to perfect love of our Lord Jesus.

Nevertheless on the other side I say also, what work
or what stirring it may be that may help thy desire,
and make thy thought furthest from lust and mind
of the world, more whole and more burning to the love
of God, strengthen it and nourish it ; whether it be
praying or thinking ; whether stillness or speaking,
reading or hearing, loneliness or communing, going
or sitting ; keep it for the time and work therein as
long as the savour lasteth, if it so be that thou take
therewith meat and drink and sleep as a pilgrim doth,

and keep discretion in thy working after counsel and ordinance of thy sovereign. For have he never so great haste in his going, yet will he eat and drink and sleep. Do thou likewise. For though it let thee one time, it shall further thee another time.

ST. CATHERINE OF GENOA

1447–1510

THE family of Fieschi into which Catherine was born was a very distinguished one which had given two popes to the Church and several illustrious men to Italy ; her father had been viceroy of Naples. At sixteen she was married to William Adorno, a bad-tempered and unscrupulous young man who led his wife an awful life. She moped for five years and for another five tried to distract herself in social life, till one day in 1474, while she was preparing for confession, she had a sudden vision in which she saw her own sinfulness and God's goodness so clearly that she lost consciousness on the spot. Thereupon she made a general confession, subjected herself to rigorous penance, and after a time was admitted to daily communion.

For fifteen years Catherine had frequent visions and revelations, her contemplation being joined to tireless work for the poor and sick ; she helped to found an association to visit them in their homes, the members wearing a mask so as not to cause embarrassment to the sensitive. She reformed her husband before his death in 1497, and herself died thirteen years later after many grievous trials and sufferings.

The treatise on Purgatory of Catherine of Genoa is one of the most famous works on the subject, and she wrote a dialogue between the soul and the body in which she treats allegorically of mankind, the spirit, self-love, our Lord, and so on.

TRANSLATIONS : *Dialogue entre l'âme et le corps. On Purgatory* (Burns Oates & Washbourne, New Edition, 1929).

THE SOULS IN PURGATORY

THE souls in purgatory, as far as I can understand the matter, cannot but choose to be there ; and this by God's ordinance, who has justly decreed it so. They cannot reflect within themselves and say, ' I have done such and such sins, for which I deserve to be here ' ; nor can they say, ' Would that I had not done them, that now I might go to Paradise ' ; nor yet say, ' That soul is going out before me ' ; nor, ' I shall go out before him.' They can remember nothing of themselves or others, whether good or evil, which might increase the pain they ordinarily endure ; they are so completely satisfied with what God has ordained for them, that He should be doing all that pleases Him, and in the way it pleases Him, that they are incapable of thinking of themselves even in the midst of their greatest sufferings. They behold only the goodness of God, Whose mercy is so great in bringing men to Himself, that they cannot see anything that may affect them, whether good or bad ; if they could, they would not be in pure charity. They do not know that their sufferings are for the sake of their sins, nor can they keep in view the sins themselves ; for in doing so there would be an act of imperfection, which could have no place where there can be no longer any possibility of actually sinning.

Once, in passing out of this life, they perceive why they have their purgatory ; but never afterwards, otherwise self would come in. Abiding, then, in charity, and not being able to deviate therefrom by any real defect, they have no will, no desire, nothing but the will of pure love ; they are in that fire of purgatory by the appointment of God, which is all one with pure love ; and they cannot in anything turn aside from it, because, as they can no more merit, so they can no more sin.

JOYS AND SUFFERINGS OF PURGATORY

I DO not believe it would be possible to find any joy
comparable to that of a soul in purgatory, except
the joy of the blessed in Paradise—a joy which goes on
increasing day by day, as God more and more flows
in upon the soul, which He does abundantly in proportion as every hindrance to His entrance is consumed
away.   The hindrance is the rust of sin ; the fire
consumes the rust, and thus the soul goes on laying
itself open to the Divine inflowing.

It is as with a covered object.   The object cannot
respond to the rays of the sun, not because the sun
ceases to shine—for it shines without intermission—
but because the covering intervenes.   Let the covering
be destroyed, again the object will be exposed to the
sun, and will answer to the rays which beat against it
in proportion as the work of destruction advances.
Thus the souls are covered by a rust—that is, sin
which is gradually consumed away by the fire of
purgatory ; the more it is consumed, the more they
respond to God, their true Sun ; their happiness
increases as the rust falls off, and lays them open to the
Divine ray ; and so their happiness grows greater
as the impediment grows less, till the time is accomplished.   The pain, however, does not diminish, but
only the time of remaining in that pain.   As far as
their will is concerned, these souls cannot acknowledge
the pain as such, so completely are they satisfied with
the ordinance of God, so entirely is their will one with
it in pure charity.   On the other hand, they suffer
a torment so extreme, that no tongue could describe it,
no intellect could form the least idea of it, if God
had not made it known by special grace ; which idea,
however, God's grace has shown my soul ; but I
cannot find words to express it with my tongue, yet
the sight of it has never left my mind.   I will describe

it as I can : they will understand it whose intellect the Lord shall vouchsafe to open.

DIVINE WISDOM MANIFESTED BY HELL AND PURGATORY

As the soul cleansed and purified finds no place wherein to rest but God, this being its end by creation, so the soul in a state of sin finds no place for it but hell, this being its end by the appointment of God. No sooner, then, does the soul leave the body in mortal sin than it goes straight to hell as to its allotted place, with no other guide than the nature of sin ; and should a soul not find itself thus prevented by the justice of God, but excluded altogether from His appointment, it would endure a still greater hell—for God's appointment partakes of His mercy, and is less severe than the sin deserves ; as it is, the soul, finding no place suited to it, nor any lesser pain provided for it by God, casts itself into hell as into its proper place. Thus, with regard to purgatory, when the soul leaves the body, and finds itself out of that state of purity in which it was created, seeing the hindrance, and that it can only be removed by purgatory, without a moment's hesitation it plunges therein : and were there no such means provided to remove the impediment, it would forthwith beget within itself a hell worse than purgatory, because by reason of this impediment it would see itself unable to reach God, its last end : and this hindrance would be so full of pain, that, in comparison with it, purgatory, though, as I have said, it be like hell, would not be worth a thought, but be even as nothing.

AGAIN I say that, on God's part, I see Paradise has no gate, but that whosoever will may enter therein ; for God is all mercy, and stands with open arms to

admit us to His glory. But still I see that the Being of
God is so pure (far more than one can imagine),
that should a soul see in itself even the least mote of
imperfection, it would rather cast itself into a thousand
hells than go with that spot into the presence of the
Divine Majesty. Therefore, seeing purgatory ordained
to take away such blemishes, it plunges therein, and
deems it a great mercy that it can thus remove them.

No tongue can express, no mind can understand,
how dreadful is purgatory. Its pain is like that of
hell ; and yet (as I have said) I see any soul with the
least stain of imperfection accept it as a mercy, not
thinking it of any moment when compared with being
kept from its Love. It appears to me that the greatest
pain the souls in purgatory endure proceeds from their
being sensible of something in themselves displeasing
to God, and that it has been done voluntarily against
so much goodness ; for, being in a state of grace,
they know the truth, and how grievous is any obstacle
which does not let them approach God.

THE LOVE OF GOD IN PURGATORY

ALL the things of which I have spoken, when compared
with that of which I am assured in my intelligence,
so far as I am able to comprehend it in this life, are
of such intensity, that, by the side of them, all things
seen, all things felt, all things imagined, all things just
and true, seem to me lies and things of naught. I am
confounded at my inability to find stronger words.
I see that God is in such perfect conformity with the
soul, that when He beholds it in the purity wherein
it was created by His Divine Majesty, He imparts
a certain attractive impulse of His burning love,
enough to annihilate it, though it be immortal ; and
in this way so transforms the soul into Himself, its
God, that it sees in itself nothing but God, who goes

on thus attracting and inflaming it, until He has brought it to that state of existence whence it came forth—that is, the spotless purity wherein it was created. And when the soul, by interior illumination, perceives that God is drawing it with such loving ardour to Himself, straightway there springs up within it a corresponding fire of love for its most sweet Lord and God, which causes it wholly to melt away : it sees in the Divine light how considerately, and with what unfailing providence, God is ever leading it to its full perfection, and that He does it all through pure love ; it finds itself stopped by sin, and unable to follow that heavenly attraction—I mean that look which God casts on it to bring it into union with Himself : and this sense of the grievousness of being kept from beholding the Divine light, coupled with that instinctive longing which would fain be without hindrance to follow the enticing look—these two things, I say, make up the pains of the souls in purgatory. Not that they think anything of their pains, however great they be ; they think far more of the opposition they are making to the will of God, which they see clearly is burning intensely with pure love to them. God meanwhile goes on drawing the soul to Himself by His looks of love mightily, and, as it were, with undivided energy : this the soul knows well ; and could it find another purgatory greater than this by which it could sooner remove so great an obstacle, it would immediately plunge therein, impelled by that conforming love which is between God and the soul.

ST. TERESA

1515–1582

TERESA was born of a noble family at Avila in Castile on March 28, 1515. She was a pious child and when she was only seven ran away from home with her little brother to seek martyrdom among the Moors. When she was sixteen she went as a boarder to the Augustinian convent at Avila, but ill-health sent her home. In 1533 she became a Carmelite at the Incarnation priory in the same town, and six years later recovered from a very serious sickness at the intercession of St. Joseph, for whom she had always a great devotion.

It was long before her fervour and perseverance were stabilized, and it was not till she was forty that she began to enter on the way of heroic sanctity. She was confirmed therein by St. Francis Borgia and St. Peter of Alcantara, and put herself under the direction of the Jesuit father Balthazar Alvarez.

The mitigated rule followed by all Carmelites at that time could not satisfy Teresa's aspirations, and in 1562 she founded, amid the greatest difficulties, the first monastery of reformed Carmelite nuns, St. Joseph's, at Avila. Here she wrote her autobiography and *The Way of Perfection*. In 1567 she founded the convent of Medina del Campo, and in the same year met for the first time St. John of the Cross, who was then less than half her own age. Together they soon established the first house of reformed friars of their order, at Duruelo.

Teresa spent the rest of her life setting up reformed convents up and down Spain, and it is difficult to know which is the more remarkable: the graces of prayer granted her by God (she experienced the 'spiritual marriage' in 1572), described by her in masterly fashion in the *Interior Castle*, or the tireless energy of her incredible activity which she chronicles in the *Book of the Foundations*. On returning from one of these apostolic journeys she fell ill and died at Alba, on October 4, 1582. She was canonized in 1662.

St. Teresa was a most powerful personality, endowed with vivid imagination and piercing intelligence. She read a lot, especially the writings of Louis of Granada, St. Peter of Alcantara, St. John Cassian, St. Vincent Ferrer, and the *Spiritual Exercises* of St. Ignatius, and translated several works from Latin into Castilian. She is easily one of the greatest mystical writers who ever lived, and her books have helped countless souls on the road to perfection. Her writing is lively, vivid, and easily understood, and she describes the highest graces and physical phenomena of mysticism in a simple straightforward way : the reader is captivated both by the books and by the writer.

TRANSLATIONS : *Life of St. Theresa of Jesus of the Order of Our Lady of Carmel.*
The Way of Perfection.
The Interior Castle or The Mansions.
(All published by The Newman Press.)

A VISION OF HELL

SOME considerable time after our Lord had bestowed upon me the graces I have been describing, and others also of a higher nature, I was one day in prayer when I found myself in a moment, without knowing how, plunged apparently into hell. I understood that it was our Lord's will I should see the place which the devils kept in readiness for me, and which I had deserved by my sins. It was but a moment, but it seems to me impossible I should ever forget it, even if I were to live many years.

The entrance seemed to be by a long narrow pass, like a furnace, very low, dark, and close. The ground seemed to be saturated with water, mere mud, exceedingly foul, sending forth pestilential odours, and covered with loathsome vermin. At the end was a hollow place in the wall, like a closet, and in that I saw myself confined. All this was even pleasant to behold in comparison with what I felt there. There is no exaggeration in what I am saying.

But as to what I then felt, I do not know where to begin, if I were to describe it ; it is utterly inexplicable. I felt a fire in my soul. I cannot see how it is possible to describe it. My bodily sufferings were unendurable. I have undergone most painful sufferings in this life, and, as the physicians say, the greatest that can be borne, such as the contraction of my sinews when I was paralysed, without speaking of others of different kinds, yea, even those of which I have also spoken, inflicted on me by Satan ; yet all these were as nothing in comparison with what I felt then, especially when I saw that there would be no intermission, nor any end to them.

These sufferings were nothing in comparison with the anguish of my soul, a sense of oppression, of stifling, and of pain so keen, accompanied by so hopeless and cruel an infliction, that I know not how to speak of it. If I said that the soul is continually being torn from the body it would be nothing—for that implies the destruction of life by the hands of another ; but here it is the soul itself that is tearing itself in pieces. I cannot describe that inward fire or that despair surpassing all torments and all pain. I did not see who it was that tormented me, but I felt myself on fire, and torn to pieces, as it seemed to me ; and, I repeat it, this inward fire and despair are the greatest torments of all.

Left in that pestilential place, and utterly without the power to hope for comfort, I could neither sit nor lie down : there was no room. I was placed as it were in a hole in the wall ; and those walls, terrible to look on of themselves, hemmed me in on every side.

I could not breathe. There was no light, but all was thick darkness. I do not understand how it is ; though there was no light, yet everything that can give pain by being seen was visible.

Our Lord at that time would not let me see more of hell. Afterwards I had another most fearful vision, in which I saw the punishment of certain sins. They were most horrible to look at ; but, because I felt none of the pain, my terror was not so great. In the former vision our Lord made me really feel I had been suffering them in the body there. I know now how it was, but I understood distinctly that it was a great mercy that our Lord would have me see with mine own eyes the very place from which His compassion saved me. I have listened to people speaking of these things, and I have at other times dwelt on the various torments of hell, though not often, because my soul made no progress by the way of fear ; and I have read of the diverse tortures, and how the devils tear the flesh with red-hot pincers. But all is as nothing before this ; it is a wholly different matter. In short, the one is a reality, the other a picture ; and all burning here in this life is as nothing in comparison with the fire that is there.

I was so terrified by that vision—and that terror is on me even now while I am writing—that though it took place nearly six years ago, the natural warmth of my body is chilled by fear even now when I think of it. And so, amid all the pain and suffering which I may have had to bear, I remember no time in which I do not think that all we have to suffer in this world is as nothing. It seems to me that we complain without reason. I repeat it, this vision was one of the grandest mercies of our Lord. It has been to me of the greatest service, because it has destroyed my fear of trouble and of the contradiction of the world, and because it has made me strong enough to bear up against them, and to give thanks to our Lord, who has been my Deliverer, as it now seems to me, from such fearful and everlasting pains.

Ever since that time, as I was saying, everything seems endurable in comparison with one instant of suffering such as those I had then to bear in hell. I am filled with fear when I see that, after frequently reading books which describe in some manner the pains of hell, I was not afraid of them, nor made any account of them.   Where was I ?   How could I possibly take any pleasure in those things which led me directly to so dreadful a place ?   Blessed for ever be Thou, O my God !   and, oh, how manifest is it that Thou didst love me much more than I did love Thee !   How often, O Lord, didst Thou save me from that fearful prison !   And how I used to get back to it contrary to Thy will.

It was that vision that filled me with the very great distress which I feel at the sight of so many lost souls, especially of the Lutherans—for they were once members of the Church by baptism—and also gave me the most vehement desires for the salvation of souls ; for certainly I believe that, to save even one from those overwhelming torments, I would most willingly endure many deaths.   If here on earth we see one whom we specially love in great trouble or pain, our very nature seems to bid us compassionate him ; and if those pains be great, we are troubled ourselves. What, then, must it be to see a soul in danger of pain, the most grievous of all pains, for ever ?   Who can endure it ?   It is a thought no heart can bear without great anguish.   Here we know that pain ends with life at last, and that there are limits to it ; yet the sight of it moves our compassion so greatly.   That other pain has no ending ; and I know not how we can be calm, when we see Satan carry so many souls daily away.

FIAT VOLUNTAS TUA

ST. TERESA makes a fine commentary on the Our Father in her *Way of Perfection*. Speaking of ' Thy will be done on earth as it is is in heaven,' she says :

I wish to remind you what is the will of God, so that you may know with whom you have to deal, as the saying goes, and may realize what the good Jesus is offering to the Father on your behalf. Know that when you say ' Thy will be done ' you are begging that God's will may be carried out in you, for it is *this*, and nothing else, for which you ask. You need not fear that He will give you riches, or pleasures, or great honours, or any earthly good—His love for you is not so lukewarm—He places a higher value on your gift and wishes to reward you generously, since He has given you His kingdom even in this life. Would you like to see how He treats those who make this petition unreservedly ? Ask His glorious Son, who in the garden uttered it truthfully and resolutely. See whether the will of God was not accomplished in the trials, the sufferings, the insults, and the persecutions sent Him, until at last His life was ended on the cross. Thus you see, daughters, what God gave to Him He loved best : this shows what His will means. These are His gifts in this world, and He grants them in proportion to His affection for us. To souls He cherishes most He gives more—and fewer to those less dear to Him, according to their courage and the love He sees they bear Him. For fervent love can suffer much for Him, while tepidity will endure but little. For my part, I believe that our love is the measure of the cross we can bear ?

Then, sisters, if you have this love, think of what you are doing : let not the promises you made to so great a God be only words of empty compliment, but force yourselves to suffer whatever God wishes.

Any other way of yielding Him our will is like offering someone a jewel, begging him to accept it, and holding it fast when he puts out his hand to take it. It is shameful to trifle thus with One who has done so much for us. Were there no other reason, it would be wrong to mock Him thus, again and again, whenever we repeat the *Pater Noster*. Let us give Him once for all the gem we have so often proffered Him— although He first gave us what we now tender to His Father.

ON NOT EXCUSING ONESELF USELESSLY

I AM overwhelmed with confusion at speaking on this subject, and I do not know how to fulfil my task. The fault is yours, sisters, for you bade me undertake the work—you must read it as best you can since I do my best to write it and you must not criticize its shortcomings. Such a book requires leisure ; as you know, I have so little that I have been unable to go on with it for a week, and I forget both what I have already written and how I intended to continue. I can do nothing but blame myself for my failings, and beg you not to imitate me by excusing yourselves as I am doing here. Not to exculpate ourselves when unjustly accused is a sublime virtue, and very edifying and meritorious ; but, although I have often taught it you, and by the mercy of God you practise it, yet His Majesty has never given me the grace to do so myself—may He grant that I do before I die ! Yet there always seems to me some good reason for thinking it would be better to make some excuse for myself. This is often lawful, indeed, sometimes it would be wrong to omit it, yet I have not sufficient discretion —or rather, humility—to know when it should be done. For indeed it requires great humility to see oneself blamed without cause, and to be silent ; we thus

imitate our Lord, who freed us from our sins. Be most
careful to act in this way, sisters; it does us great
good, while I can see no use in our exculpating ourselves, unless, as I said, when we might cause offence
or scandal by not telling the truth. Anyone who is
more prudent than I am will easily understand this.
I think it is a great gain to accustom oneself to practise
this virtue, and to endeavour to obtain from God the
true humility that must be the result. Whoever is
really humble ought to wish sincerely to be despised,
persecuted, and condemned for serious offences without
any just cause. If you seek to follow our Lord, in
what better way can you do so? No bodily strength
is needed here, nor the help of any one save God.

I wish these great virtues, my sisters, to be both
our study and our penance. You know that I restrain
you from other severe and excessive austerities, which
if performed imprudently might injure your health.
Here, however, there is nothing to fear; for, however
great the interior virtues may be, they do not weaken
the body so that it cannot keep the Rule of the religious
life. These strengthen the soul, and, as I have often
told you by constantly conquering yourselves in little
things, you may train yourselves to gain the victory
in great matters. But—how well I have written this,
and how badly I practise it!—indeed, I have never
been tried thus in any important affair, for I never
heard any ill spoken of me that did not fall far short
of the truth, if not in that particular matter, yet often
enough in similar things: only too often in other ways
have I offended our Lord God, and I thought people
showed me a great kindness in not speaking of these.
I always prefer that they should find fault with what
I have not done, for the truth is very painful to hear;
but for a false accusation, however grave, I care
nothing, and in minor matters I follow my natural
bent without thinking of what is most perfect. For
this reason, I wish you to understand from the first,

and I desire each one of you to consider, how much is gained by this habit of not excusing yourselves. I think it can never do any harm, while its chief advantage is that we thus, to a certain degree, imitate our Lord. I say, 'to a certain degree,' for we are never wholly innocent when blamed, but are always guilty of many sins, for 'the just man falleth seven times a day,' and 'if we say we have no sin, the truth is not in us'; therefore, though we may not be guilty of this particular fault, yet we are never altogether free from offence as was the good Jesus.

O my Lord, when I remember in how many ways Thou didst suffer, who yet in no way didst deserve it, I know not what to say for myself, nor of what I am thinking when I shrink from suffering or defend myself from blame! Thou knowest, O my only God! that if there is aught that is right in me it comes from Thy hands. Why shouldst Thou not give me much instead of little? If it is because I do not deserve it, neither have I deserved the graces Thou hast already bestowed on me. Can it be that I should wish men to think well of a thing so vile as I am, when they said such evil things of Thee, who art above every other good? Do not permit this: forbid it, O my God! Nor let me wish that anything displeasing to Thine eyes should be found in me, Thy handmaiden. See, O my Lord! I am blind and I care but little for the light. Enlighten me and make me sincerely desire that all men should hate me, since I have so often abandoned Thee who lovest me so faithfully. Why do we act thus, O my God? What joy do we think to find by pleasing creatures? What does it matter of what guilt they accuse us if we are guiltless before Thee, O Lord?

DELIGHTS OF PASSIVE LOVE

NOT long afterwards His Majesty began, according
to His promise, to make it clear that it was He Himself
who appeared, by the growth in me of the love of
God so strong, that I knew not who could have
infused it ; for it was most supernatural, and I had
not attained to it by any efforts of my own. I saw
myself dying with a desire to see God, and I knew
not how to seek that life otherwise than by dying.
Certain great impetuosities of love, though not so
intolerable as those of which I have spoken before,
nor yet of so great worth, overwhelmed me. I knew
not what to do ; for nothing gave me pleasure, and
I had no control over myself. Oh, supreme artifice
of our Lord ! How tenderly didst Thou deal with
Thy miserable slave ! Thou didst hide Thyself from
me, and didst yet constrain me with Thy love, with
a death so sweet, that my soul would never wish it over.

It is not possible for any one to understand these
impetuosities if he has not experienced them himself.
They are not an upheaving of the breast, nor those
devotional sensations, not uncommon, which seem on
the point of causing suffocation, and are beyond
control. That prayer is of a much lower order ;
and those agitations should be avoided by gently
endeavouring to be recollected ; and the soul should
be kept in quiet. . . .

These other impetuosities are very different. It
is not we who apply the fuel ; the fire is already
kindled, and we are thrown into it in a moment to be
consumed. It is by no efforts of the soul that it
sorrows over the wound which the absence of our
Lord has inflicted on it ; it is far otherwise ; for an
arrow is driven into the entrails to the very quick,
and into the heart at times, so that the soul knows
not what is the matter with it, not what it wishes for.

It understands clearly enough that it wishes for God, and that the arrow seems tempered with some herb which makes the soul hate itself for the love of our Lord, and willingly lose its life for Him. It is impossible to describe or explain the way in which God wounds the soul, or the very grievous pain inflicted, which deprives it of all self-consciousness ; yet this pain is so sweet, that there is no joy in the world which gives greater delight. And I have just said, the soul would wish to be always dying of this wound.

This pain and bliss together carried me out of myself, and I never could understand how it was. Oh, what a sight a wounded soul is !—a soul, I mean, so conscious of it as to be able to say of itself that it is wounded for so good a cause ; and seeing distinctly that it never did anything whereby this love should come to it, and that it does come from that exceeding love which our Lord bears it. A spark seems to have fallen suddenly upon it, that has set it all on fire. Oh, how often do I remember, when in this state, those words of David : ' *Quemadmodum desiderat cervus a fontes aquarun !* ' They seem to me to be literally true of myself.

When these impetuosities are not very violent they seem to admit of a little mitigation—at least, the soul seeks some relief, because it knows not what to do—through certain penances ; the painfulness of which, and even the shedding of its blood, are no more felt than if the body were dead. The soul seeks for ways and means to do something that may be felt, for the love of God ; but the first pain is so great, that no bodily torture I know of can take it away. As relief is not to be had here, these medicines are too mean for so high a disease. Some slight mitigation may be had, and the pain may pass away a little, by praying God to relieve its sufferings, but the soul sees no relief except in death, by which it thinks to attain completely to the fruition of its good.

PRAYER OF UNION :
THE MYSTICAL BUTTERFLY

You have heard how wonderfully silk is made—in a way such as God alone could plan—how it all comes from an egg resembling a tiny pepper-corn. Not having seen it myself, I only know of it by hearsay, so if the facts are inaccurate the fault will not be mine. When, in the warm weather, the mulberry trees come into leaf, the little egg which was lifeless before its food was ready, begins to live. The caterpillar nourishes itself upon the mulberry leaves until, when it has grown large, people place near it small twigs upon which, of its own accord, it spins silk from its tiny mouth until it has made a narrow little cocoon in which it buries itself. Then this large and ugly worm leaves the cocoon as a lovely little white butterfly.

If we had not seen this, but had only heard of it as an old legend, who could believe it ? Could we persuade ourselves that insects so utterly without the use of reason as a silkworm or a bee would work with such industry and skill in our service that the poor little silkworm loses its life over the task ? This would suffice for a short meditation, sisters, without my adding more, for you may learn from it the wonders and the wisdom of God. How if we knew the properties of all things ? It is most profitable to ponder over the grandeurs of creation and to exult in being the brides of such a wise and mighty King.

Let us return to our subject. The silkworm symbolizes the soul which begins to live when, kindled by the Holy Spirit, it commences using the ordinary aids given by God to all, and applies the remedies left by Him in His Church, such as regular confession, religious books, and sermons ; these are the cure for a soul dead in its negligence and sins and liable to fall into temptation. Then it comes to life and continues nourishing itself on this food and on devout meditation until it has attained full vigour, which is the essential point, for I attach no importance to the rest. When the silkworm is full grown, as I told you in the first part of this chapter, it begins to spin silk and to build the house wherein it must die. By this house, when speaking of the soul, I mean Christ. I think I heard or read somewhere, either that our life is hid in Christ, or in God (which means the same thing), or that Christ is our life. It makes little difference to my meaning which of these quotations is correct. . . .

Forward then, my daughters ! Hasten over your work and build the little cocoon. Let us renounce self-love and self-will, care for nothing earthly, do penance, pray, mortify ourselves, be obedient, and perform all the other good works of which you know. Act up to your light ; you have been taught your duties. Die ! Die as the silkworm does when it has fulfilled the office of its creation, and you will see God and be immersed in His greatness, as the little silkworm is enveloped in its cocoon. Understand that when I say ' you will see God,' I mean in the manner described, in which He manifests Himself in this kind of union.

Now let us see what becomes of the ' silkworm,' for all I have been saying leads to this. As soon as by means of this prayer the soul has become entirely dead to the world, it comes forth like a lovely little white butterfly ! Oh, how great God is ! How beautiful is the soul after having been immersed in God's grandeur and united closely to Him for but a short time ! Indeed, I do not think it is ever so long as half an hour. Truly, the spirit does not recognize itself, being as different from what it was as is the white butterfly from the repulsive caterpillar. It does not know how it can have merited so great a good, or rather, whence this grace came which it well knows it merits not. The soul desires to praise our Lord God and longs to sacrifice and die a thousand deaths for Him. It feels an unconquerable desire for great crosses and would like to perform the most severe penances ; it sighs for solitude and would have all men know God, while it is bitterly grieved at seeing them offend HIM. These matters will be described more fully in the next mansion ; there they are of the same nature, yet in a more advanced state the effects are stronger, because, as I told you, if, after the soul has received these favours, it strives to make still further progress, it will experience great things.

GOD'S CONTINUAL PRESENCE

When our Lord is pleased to take pity on the sufferings, both past and present, endured through her longing for Him by this soul which He has spiritually taken for His bride, He, before consummating the celestial marriage, brings her into this His mansion or presence-chamber. This is the seventh mansion, for as He has a dwelling-place in heaven, so has He in the soul, where none but He may abide and which may be termed a second heaven. . . .

You must not think of the soul as insignificant and petty, but as an interior world containing the number of beautiful mansions you have seen ; as indeed it should, since in the centre of the soul there is a mansion reserved for God Himself.

When His Majesty deigns to bestow on the soul the grace of these Divine nuptials, He brings it into His presence-chamber and does not treat it as before. . . .

By some mysterious manifestation of the truth, the three Persons of the most Blessed Trinity reveal themselves, preceded by an illumination which shines on the spirit like a most dazzling cloud of light. The three Persons are distinct from one another ; a sublime knowledge is infused into the soul, imbuing it with a certainty of the truth that the Three are of one substance, power, and knowledge, and are one God. Thus that which we hold as a doctrine of faith, the soul now, so to speak, understands by sight, though it beholds the blessed Trinity neither by the eyes of the body nor of the soul, this being no imaginary vision. All the Three Persons here communicate Themselves to the soul, speak to it and make it understand the words of our Lord in the Gospel that He and the Father and the Holy Ghost will come and make their abode with the soul which loves Him and keeps His commandments.

O my God, how different from merely hearing and believing these words is it to realize their truth in this way ! Day by day a growing astonishment takes possession of this soul, for the Three Persons of the Blessed Trinity seem never to depart ; it sees with certainty, in the way I have described, that They dwell far within its own centre and depths ; though for want of learning it cannot describe how it is conscious of the indwelling of these Divine Companions.

You may fancy that such a person is beside herself and that her mind is too inebriated to care for anything else. On the contrary she is far more active than before in all that concerns God's service, and when at leisure she enjoys this blessed companionship. Unless she first deserts God I believe He will never cease to make her clearly sensible of His presence : she feels confident, as indeed she may, that He will never so fail her as to allow her to lose this favour after once bestowing it ; at the same time, she is more careful than before to avoid offending Him in any way.

This presence is not always so entirely realized, that is, so distinctly manifest, as at first, or as it is at times when God renews this favour, otherwise the recipient could not possibly attend to anything else nor live in society. Although not always seen by so clear a light, yet whenever she reflects on it she feels the companionship of the Blessed Trinity. This is as if, when we were with other people in a very well lighted room, someone were to darken it by closing the shutters ; we should feel certain that the others were still there, though we were unable to see them.

You may ask : ' Could she not bring back the light and see them again ? ' This is not in her power ; when our Lord chooses, He will open the shutters of the understanding : He shows her great mercy in never quitting her and in making her realize it so clearly. His Divine Majesty seems to be preparing His bride for greater things by this Divine companionship which clearly helps perfection in every way and makes her lose the fear she sometimes felt when other graces were granted her.

A certain person so favoured found she had improved in all virtues whatever were her trials or labours, the centre of her soul seemed never moved from its resting-place. Thus in a manner her soul appeared divided : a short time after God had done for her this favour, while undergoing great sufferings, she complained of her soul as Martha did of Mary, reproaching it with enjoying solitary peace while leaving her so full of troubles and occupations that she could not keep it company.

ST. JOHN OF THE CROSS
1542–1591

John's father, Gonzalez de Yepes, was a ruined nobleman who earned his living as a weaver at Fontiberos in Castile, and his boyhood was poor and arduous. He became an infirmarian at the hospital of Medina, and in the time he could spare from the sick attended classes at the Jesuit college. When he was twenty-one he became a Carmelite, taking the name of John of St. Mathias. After his novitiate he was sent to the university of Salamanca, where he studied for four years and acquired the knowledge of the Bible, the scholastic discipline, and the solid precise style which are displayed in his writings, and he read the German and Flemish mystics assiduously.

While still there, and thinking of seeking an austerer life among the Carthusians, he met St. Teresa, who fired him with her enthusiasm for the reform of the Carmelites. Together they founded the first house of reformed friars at Duruelo, and he changed his name to John of the Cross. A conflict then broke out between the two parties in the order, and John was imprisoned ; he escaped miraculously at the end of nine months, after undergoing scandalous ill-treatment. He was then prior at several places, but continued to suffer persecution. One day at Segovia he heard our Lord ask him, ' John, what reward do you look for from your labours ? ' ' Lord,' he replied, ' To suffer hardship and contempt for Your sake.'

St. John attained to the sublime state of ' spiritual marriage ' and his union with God was complete and constant. St. Teresa said of him : ' One cannot talk about God with Father John, for he goes into ecstasy at once and makes others do the same.' He died at Ubeda in 1591, aged only forty-nine.

St. John is *the* mystical doctor of the Church, and from

the psychological side he is unrivalled. One of his great achievements is to have made clear what he calls the ' dark night of the senses,' the way by which the soul passes from meditation to infused contemplation ; he was the first to distinguish and describe the great mystical trials as the ' dark night of the senses ' and the ' dark night of the soul.' In *The Ascent of Mount Carmel* he describes how to reach the summit of perfection, and the necessary perfect mortification of body and spirit is presented under the figure of might. But this might is double : the active might is the mortification which the soul imposes on herself, and this is described in *The Ascent of Mount Carmel* ; passive might is the far more intense purification with which God visits the soul in various ways, and St. John deals with this in *The Dark Night*. He distinguishes the two purifications as the ' dark night of the senses,' which leads to mystical contemplation, and the yet more terrible ' dark night of the soul,' which precedes the height of union. In *The Spiritual Canticle* and *The Living Flame of Love* he is concerned with the blessed condition of the soul in the perfect union of love and the divinization of all her faculties.

TRANSLATIONS: *The Complete Works of St. John of the Cross*. (The Newman Press, 1945.)

The Burning Soul of St. John of the Cross. By Rodolphe Hoornaert. Translated by Algar Thorold. (Burns Oates & Washbourne, 1931).

Life of St. John of the Cross. By Father Bruno, O.C.D. (London, 1932).

COMPLETE MORTIFICATION NECESSARY FOR DIVINE UNION

1. THE reason for which it is necessary for the soul, in order to attain Divine union with God, to pass through this dark night of mortification of the desires and denial of pleasures in all things, is because all the affections which it has for creatures are pure darkness in the eyes of God, and, when the soul is clothed in

these affections, it has no capacity for being enlightened and possessed by the pure and simple light of God if it cast them not first from it ; for the light cannot agree with darkness ; since, as St. John says : *Tenebræ eam non comprehenderunt.* That is : The darkness could not receive the light.

2. The reason is that two contraries (even as philosophy teaches us) cannot coexist in one person ; and that darkness, which is affection for the creatures, and light, which is God, are contrary to each other, and have no likeness nor accord between one another, even as St. Paul explained to the Corinthians, saying : *Quæ conventio luci ad tenebras ?* That is to say : What communion can there be between light and darkness ? Hence it is that the light of Divine union cannot dwell in the soul if these affections first flee not away from it.

3. In order that we may the better prove what has been said, it must be known that the affection and attachment which the soul has for creatures renders the soul like to these creatures ; and the greater is its affection, the closer is the equality and likeness between them ; for love creates a likeness between that which loves and that which is loved. For which reason David, speaking of those who set their affections upon idols, said thus : *Similes illis fiant qui faciunt ea : et omnes qui confidunt in eis.* Which signifies : Let them that set their heart upon them be like to them. And thus he that loves a creature becomes as low as is that creature, and, in some ways, lower ; for love not only makes the lover equal to the object of his love, but even subjects him to it. Wherefore in the same wa, it comes to pass that the soul that loves anything else becomes incapable of pure union with God and transformation in Him. For the low estate of the creature is much less capable of union with the high estate of the Creator than is darkness with light. For all things of earth and heaven, compared with God, are nothing, as Jeremiah says in these words : *Aspexi*

*terram, et ecce vacua erat, et nihil ; et coelos, et non erat
lux in eis.* I beheld the earth, he says, and it was void,
and it was nothing ; and the heavens, and saw that
they had no light. In saying that he beheld the earth
void, he means that all its creatures were nothing,
and that the earth was nothing likewise. And, in
saying that he beheld the heavens and saw no light
in them, he says that all the luminaries of heaven,
compared with God, are pure darkness. So that in
this sense, all the creatures are nothing ; and their
affections, we may say, are less than nothing, since they
are an impediment to transformation in God and the
loss thereof, even as darkness is not only nothing,
but less than nothing, since it is loss of light. And
even as he that is in darkness comprehends not the
light, so the soul that sets its affections upon creatures
will be unable to comprehend God ; and, until it be
purged, it will neither be able to possess Him here
below, through pure transformation of love, nor
yonder in clear vision. And, for greater clarity, we
will now speak in greater detail.

4. All the being of creation, then, compared with the
infinite being of God, is nothing. And therefore the
soul that sets its affections upon the being of creation
is likewise nothing in the eyes of God, and less than
nothing ; for, as we have said, love makes equality
and similitude, and even sets the lover below the object
of his love. And therefore such a soul will in no wise
be able to attain to union with the infinite being of
God ; for that which is not can have no agreement
with that which is. And, coming down in detail
to certain examples, all the beauty of the creatures,
compared with the infinite beauty of God, is the
height of deformity, even as Solomon says in the
Proverbs : *Fallax gratia, et vana est pulchritudo.* Favour
is deceitful and beauty is vain. And thus the soul that
is affectioned to the beauty of any creature is as the
height of deformity in the eyes of God. And therefore

the soul that is deformed will be unable to become transformed in beauty, which is God, since deformity cannot attain to beauty ; and all the grace and beauty of the creatures, compared with the grace of God, is the height of misery and of unattractiveness. Wherefore the soul that is ravished by the graces and beauties of the creatures has only supreme misery and unattractiveness in the eyes of God ; and thus it cannot be capable of the infinite grace and loveliness of God ; for that which has no grace is far removed from that which is infinitely gracious ; and all the goodness of the creatures of the world, in comparison with the infinite goodness of God, may be described as wickedness. For there is naught good, save only God. And therefore the soul that sets its heart upon the good things of the world is supremely evil in the eyes of God. And, even as wickedness comprehends not goodness, even so much a soul cannot be united with God, who is supreme goodness. All the wisdom of the world and human ability, compared with the infinite wisdom of God, are pure and supreme ignorance, even as St. Paul writes *ad Corinthios*, saying : *Sapientia hujus mundi stultitia est apud Deum.* The wisdom of this world is foolishness in the eyes of God.

5. Wherefore any soul that makes account of all its knowledge and ability in order to come to union with the wisdom of God, is supremely ignorant in the eyes of God and will remain far removed from that wisdom ; for ignorance knows not what wisdom is, even as St. Paul says that this wisdom seems foolishness to God.

6. Wherefore the soul that is enamoured of prelacy, or of any other such office, and longs for liberty of desire, is considered and treated, in the sight of God, not as a son, but as a base slave and captive, since it has not been willing to accept His holy doctrine, wherein He teaches us that he who would be greater must be less, and he who would be less must be greater.

And therefore such a soul will be unable to attain to that true liberty of spirit which is encompassed in His Divine union. For slavery can have no part with liberty; and liberty cannot dwell in a heart that is subject to desires, for this is the heart of a slave; but it dwells in the free man, because he has the heart of a son. It was for this reason that Sarah bade her husband Abraham cast out the bond-woman and her son, saying that the son of the bondwoman should not be heir with the son of the free woman.

7. And all the delights and pleasures of the will in all the things of the world, in comparison with all those delights which are God, are supreme affliction, torment and bitterness. And thus he that sets his heart upon them is considered in the sight of God, as worthy of supreme affliction, torment and bitterness; and thus he will be unable to attain to the delights of the embrace of union with God, since he is worthy of affliction and bitterness. All the wealth and glory of all the creatures, in comparison with the wealth which is God, is supreme poverty and wretchedness. Thus the soul that loves and possesses creature wealth is supremely poor and wretched in the sight of God, and for this reason he will be unable to attain to that wealth and glory which is the state of transformation in God; since that which is miserable and poor is supremely far removed from that which is supremely rich and glorious.

SPIRITUAL WISDOM

—*In order to arrive at having pleasure in everything,*
Desire to have pleasure in nothing.
—*In order to arrive at possessing everything,*
Desire to possess nothing.
—*In order to arrive at being everything,*
Desire to be nothing.

—In order to arrive at a knowledge of everything,
Desire to know nothing.
—In order to arrive at that wherein thou hast no pleasure,
Thou must go by a way wherein thou hast no pleasure.
—In order to arrive at that which thou knowest not,
Thou must go by a way that thou knowest not.
—In order to arrive at that which thou possessest not,
Thou must go by a way that thou possessest not.
—In order to arrive at that which thou art not,
Thou must go through that which thou art not.

HINDERING CONTEMPLATION

A FAVOURITE theme with St. John is the importance
for those whom God has led to contemplation not to
hinder it by the activity of their reasoning and
imaginative powers.

6. Great, therefore, is the error of many spiritual
persons who have practised approaching God by
means of images and forms and meditations, as befits
beginners. God would now lead them on to further
spiritual blessings, which are interior and invisible, by
taking from them the pleasure and sweetness of dis-
cursive meditation ; but they cannot, or dare not,
or know not how to detach themselves from those
palpable methods to which they have grown
accustomed. They continually labour to retain them,
desiring to proceed, as before, by the way of consideration and meditation upon forms, for they think
that it must be so with them always. They labour
greatly to this end and find little sweetness or none ;
rather the aridity and weariness and disquiet of their
souls are increased and grow, in proportion as they
labour for that earlier sweetness. They cannot find
this in that earlier manner, for the soul no longer
enjoys that food of sense, as we have said ; it needs
not this, but another food, which is more delicate,
more interior and partaking less of the nature of sense ;

it consists not in labouring with the imagination, but in setting the soul at rest, and allowing it to remain in its quiet and repose, which is more spiritual. For, the farther the soul progresses in spirituality, the more it ceases from the operation of the faculties in particular acts, for it becomes more and more occupied in one act that is general and pure ; and thus the faculties that were journeying to a place whither the soul has arrived cease to work, even as the feet stop and cease to move when their journey is over. For if all were motion, one would never arrive, and if all were means, where or when would come the fruition of the end and goal ?

7. It is piteous, then, to see many a one who, though his soul would fain tarry in this peace and rest of interior quiet, where it is filled with the peace and refreshment of God, takes from it its tranquillity, and leads it away to the most exterior things, and would make it return and retrace the ground it has already traversed, to no purpose, and abandon the end and goal wherein it is already reposing for the means which led it to that repose, which are meditations. This comes not to pass without great reluctance and repugnance of the soul, which would fain be in that peace that it understands not, as in its proper place even as one who has arrived, with great labour, and is now resting, feels pain if they make him return to his labour. And, as such souls know not the mystery of this new experience, the idea comes to them that they are being idle and doing nothing ; and thus they allow not themselves to be quiet, but endeavour to meditate and reason. Hence they are filled with aridity and affliction, because they seek to find sweetness where it is no longer to be found ; we may even say of them that the more they strive the less they profit, for, the more they persist after this manner, the worse is the state wherein they find themselves, because their soul is drawn farther away from spiritual

peace ; and this is to leave the greater for the less, and to retrace the road already traversed, and to seek to do that which has been done.

8. To such as these the advice must be given to learn to abide attentively and wait lovingly upon God in that state of quiet, and to pay no heed either to imagination or to its working ; for here, as we say, the faculties are at rest, and are working, not actively, but passively, by receiving that which God works in them ; and, if they work at times, it is not with violence or with carefully elaborated meditation, but with sweetness of love, moved less by the ability of the soul itself than by God, as will be explained hereafter.

THE TWO MYSTICAL NIGHTS

1. This night, which, as we say, is contemplation, produces in spiritual persons two kinds of darkness or purgation, corresponding to the two parts of man's nature—namely, the sensual and the spiritual. And thus the one night or purgation will be sensual, wherein the soul is purged according to sense, which is subdued to the spirit ; and the other is a night or purgation which is spiritual ; wherein the soul is purged and stripped according to the spirit, and subdued and made ready for the union of love with God. The night of sense is common and comes to many ; these are the beginners ; and of this night we shall first speak. The night of the spirit is the portion to very few, and these are they that are already practised and proficient, of whom we shall treat hereafter.

2. The first purgation or night is bitter and terrible to sense, as we shall now show. The second bears no comparison with it, for it is horrible and awful to the spirit, as we shall show presently. Since the night of sense is first in order and comes first, we shall first of all say something about it briefly, since more is written

of it, as of a thing that is more common ; and we shall pass on to treat more fully of the spiritual night, since very little has been said of this, either in speech or in writing, and very little is known of it, even by experience.

THE NIGHT OF THE SENSES : WHAT IT IS

3. SINCE, then, the conduct of these beginners upon the way of God is ignoble, and has much to do with their love of self and their own inclinations, as has been explained above, God desires to lead them farther. He seeks to bring them out of that ignoble kind of love to a higher degree of love for Him, to free them from the ignoble exercises of sense and meditation (wherewith, as we have said, they go seeking God so unworthily and in so many ways that are befitting), and to lead them to a kind of spiritual exercise wherein they can commune with Him more abundantly and are freed more completely from imperfections. For they have now had practice for some time in the way of virtue and have persevered in meditation and prayer, whereby, through the sweetness and pleasure that they have found therein, they have lost their love of the things of the world and have gained some degree of spiritual strength in God ; this has enabled them to some extent to refrain from creature desires, so that for God's sake they are now able to suffer a light burden and a little aridity without turning back to a time which they found more pleasant. When they are going about these spiritual exercises with the greatest delight and pleasure, and when they believe that the sun of Divine favour is shining most brightly upon them, God turns all this light of theirs into darkness, and shuts against them the door and the source of the sweet spiritual water which they were tasting in God whensoever and for as long as they

desired. (For, as they were weak and tender, there was no door closed to them, as St. John says in the Apocalypse, iii, 8.) And thus He leaves them so completely in the dark that they know not whither to go with their sensible imagination and meditation; for they cannot advance a step in meditation, as they were wont to do aforetime, their inward senses being submerged in this night, and left with such dryness that not only do they experience no pleasure and consolation in the spiritual things and good exercises wherein they were wont to find their delights and pleasures, but instead, on the contrary, they find insipidity and bitterness in the said things; for, as I have said, God now sees that they have grown a little, and are becoming strong enough to lay aside their swaddling clothes and be taken from the gentle breast; so He sets them down from His arms and teaches them to walk on their own feet; which they feel to be very strange, for everything seems to be going wrong with them.

4. To recollected persons this commonly happens sooner after their beginnings than to others, inasmuch as they are freer from occasions of backsliding, and their desires turn more quickly from the things of the world, which is what is needful if they are to begin to enter this blessed night of sense. Ordinarily no great time passes after their beginnings before they begin to enter this night of sense; and the great majority of them do in fact enter it, for they will generally be seen to fall into these aridities.

5. With regard to this way of purgation of the senses, since it is so common, we might here adduce a great number of quotations from Divine Scripture, where many passages relating to it are continually found, particularly in the Psalms and the Prophets. However, I do not wish to spend time upon this, for he that cannot see them there will find the common experience of them to be sufficient.

SIGNS OF THE NIGHT OF THE SENSES

1. But since these aridities might frequently proceed, not from the night and purgation of the sensual desires aforementioned, but from sins and imperfections, or from weakness and lukewarmness, or from some bad humour or indisposition of the body, I shall here set down certain signs by which it may be known if this aridity proceeds from the aforementioned purgation, or if it arises from any of the aforementioned sins. For the making of this distinction I find that there are three principal signs.

2. The first is whether, when a soul finds no pleasure or consolation in the things of God, it also fails to find it in any thing created ; for, as God sets the soul in this dark night to the end that He may quench and purge its sensual desire, He allows it not to find attraction or sweetness in anything whatsoever. Hence it may be laid down as very probable that this aridity and insipidity proceed not from recently committed sins or imperfections. For, if this were so, the soul would feel in its nature some inclination or desire to taste other things than those of God ; for, whenever the desire is allowed indulgence in any imperfection, it immediately feels inclined thereto, whether little or much, in proportion to the pleasure and the love that it had for it. Since, however, this lack of enjoyment in things above or below might proceed from some indisposition or melancholy humour, which oftentimes makes it impossible for the soul to take pleasure in anything, it becomes necessary to apply the second sign and condition.

3. The second sign whereby a man may believe himself to be experiencing the said purgation is that ordinarily the memory is centred upon God, with painful care and solicitude, thinking that it is not serving God, but is backsliding, because it finds itself

without sweetness in the things of God. And in such a case it is evident that this lack of sweetness and this aridity come not from weakness and lukewarmness ; for it is the nature of lukewarmness not to care greatly or to have any inward solicitude for the things of God. There is thus a great difference between aridity and lukewarmness, for lukewarmness consists in great weakness and remissness in will and in the spirit, without solicitude as to serving God ; whereas purgative aridity is ordinarily accompanied by solicitude, with care and grief, as I say, because the soul is not serving God.

4. The third sign whereby this purgation of sense may be recognized is that the soul can no longer meditate or reflect in its sense of the imagination, as it was wont, however much it may of itself endeavour to do so. For God now begins to communicate Himself to it, no longer through sense, as He did aforetime, by means of reflections which joined and sundered its knowledge, but by pure spirit, into which consecutive reflections enter not ; but He communicates Himself to it by an act of simple contemplation, to which neither the exterior nor the interior senses of the lower part of the soul can attain. From this time forward, therefore, imagination and fancy can find no support in any meditation, and can gain no foothold by means thereof.

THE NIGHT OF THE SOUL

THE following passages are extracted from St. John's long account of the terrible sufferings of this state.

In the first place, because the light and wisdom of this contemplation is most bright and pure, and the soul which it assails is dark and impure, it follows that the soul suffers great pain when it receives it in itself, just as, when the eyes are dimmed by humours, and become impure and weak, they suffer pain through the assault of the bright light. And when the soul is indeed assailed by this Divine light, its pain, which results from its impurity, is immense ; because, when this pure light assails the soul, in order to expel its impurity, the soul feels itself to be so impure and miserable that it believes God to be against it, and thinks that it has set itself up against God. This causes it so much grief and pain (because it now believes that God has cast it away), that one of the greatest trials which Job felt when God sent him this experience, was as follows, when he said : Why hast Thou set me against Thee, so that I am grievous and burdensome to myself? For, by means of this pure light, the soul now sees it impurity clearly (although darkly), and knows clearly that it is unworthy of God or of any creature. And what gives it most pain is that it thinks that it will never be worthy and that its good things are all over for it. This is caused by the profound immersion of its spirit in the knowledge and realization of its evils and miseries ; for this Divine and dark light now reveals them all to the eye, that it may see clearly how in its own strength it can never have aught else. In this sense we may understand that passage from David, which says : For iniquity Thou hast corrected man and hast undone his soul : he consumes away as the spider.

THE NIGHT OF THE SOUL EXPLAINED BY A COMPARISON

THE dark and hidden contemplation in this state brings extraordinary sufferings and a complete stripping bare of the soul's imperfections ; when she is cleansed, the state becomes peaceful and happy. St. John explains this by a well-known comparison.

But there is another thing here which afflicts and

distresses the soul greatly, which is that, as this dark
night has hindered its faculties and affections in this
way, it is unable to raise its affection or its mind to
God, neither can it pray to Him, thinking as Jeremias
thought concerning himself, that God has set a cloud
before it through which its prayer cannot pass. For
it is this that is meant by that which is said in the
passage referred to, namely : He hath shut and
enclosed my ways with square stones. And if it
sometimes prays it does so with such lack of strength
and of sweetness that it thinks that God neither hears
it nor pays heed to it, as this prophet likewise declares
in the same passage, saying : When I cry and entreat,
He hath cast out my prayer. In truth this is no
time for the soul to speak with God ; it should rather
put its mouth in the dust, as Jeremias says, so that
perchance there may come to it some present hope,
and it may endure its purgation with patience. It is
God who is passively working here in the soul ;
wherefore the soul can do nothing. Hence it can
neither pray nor be present at the Divine offices and
pay attention to them, much less can it attend to
other things and affairs which are temporal. Not
only so, but it has likewise such distractions and times
of such profound forgetfulness of the memory, that
frequent periods pass by without its knowing what it
has been doing or thinking, or what it is that it is
doing or is going to do, neither can it pay attention,
although it desire to do so, to anything that occupies it.

DESIRE OF UNION

IN *The Spiritual Canticle* St. John expounds one of his
poems stanza by stanza. Here is the explanation of
the sixth stanza wherein the loving soul longs ardently
for union.

1. For the greater clearness of what has been said,

and of what has still to be said, it is well to observe
at this point that this purgative and loving knowledge
or Divine light whereof we here speak acts upon the
soul which is purged and prepared for perfect union
with it in the same way as fire acts upon a log of wood
in order to transform it into itself ; for material fire,
acting upon wood, first of all begins to dry it, by driving
out its moisture and causing it to shed the water which
it contains within itself. Then it begins to make it
black, dark, and unsightly, and even to give forth
a bad odour, and, as it dries it little by little, it brings
out and drives away all the dark and unsightly
accidents which are contrary to the nature of fire.
And, finally, it begins to kindle it externally and give
it heat, and at last transforms it into itself and makes
it as beautiful as fire. In this respect, the wood has
neither passivity nor activity of its own, save for its
weight, which is greater, and its substance, which
is denser than that of fire, for it has in itself the
properties and actions of fire. Thus it is dry and it
dries ; it is hot and heats ; it is bright and gives
brightness ; and it is much less heavy than before.
All these properties and effects are caused in it by
the fire.

2. In this same way we have to philosophize with
respect to this Divine fire of contemplative love,
which, before it unites and transforms the soul in
itself, first purges it of all its contrary accidents. It
drives out its unsightliness, and makes it black and
dark, so that it seems worse than before and more
unsightly and abominable than it was wont to be.
For this Divine purgation is removing all the evil
and vicious humours which the soul has never perceived because they have been so deeply rooted and
grounded in it ; it has never realized, in fact, that it
has had so much evil within itself. But now that they
are to be driven forth and annihilated, these humours
reveal themselves, and become visible to the soul

because it is so brightly illumined by this dark light of Divine contemplation (although it is no worse than before, either in itself or in relation to God) ; and, as it sees in itself that which it saw not before, it is clear to it that it is not only unfit for God to see it, but that it deserves His abhorrence and that He does indeed abhor it.

GOD HIDDEN IN THE SOUL

5. But, besides all this, speaking now somewhat according to the sense and the affection of contemplation, in the vivid contemplation and knowledge of the creatures, the soul sees with great clearness that there is in them such abundance of graces and virtues and beauty wherewith God endowed them, that, as it seems to her, they are all clothed with marvellous natural beauty, derived from and communicated by that infinite supernatural beauty of the image of God, whose beholding of them clothes the world and all the heavens with beauty and joy ; just as does also the opening of His hand, whereby, as David says : *Imples omne animal benedictione.* That is to say : Thou fillest every animal with blessing. And therefore the soul, being wounded in love by this trace of the beauty of her Beloved which she has known in the creatures, yearns to behold that invisible beauty, and speaks as in the stanza following.

Stanza VI

Ah, who will be able to heal me ! Surrender thou thyself now completely.
From to-day do thou send me now no other messenger. For they cannot tell me what I wish.

EXPOSITION

1. As the creatures have given the soul signs of her Beloved, by revealing to her in themselves traces of

His beauty and excellence, her love has increased, and in consequence the pain which she feels at His absence has grown (for the more the soul knows of God, the more grows her desire to see Him) ; and when she sees that there is naught that can cure her pain save the sight and the presence of her Beloved, she mistrusts any other remedy, and in this stanza begs Him for the surrender and possession of His presence, entreating Him from that day forth to entertain her with no other knowledge and communications from Himself, since these satisfy not her desire and will, which is contented with naught less than the sight and presence of Him. Wherefore, she says, let Him be pleased to surrender Himself in truth, in complete and perfect love, and thus she says :

Ah, who will be able to heal me !

2. As though she had said : Among all the delights of the world and the satisfaction of the senses, and the pleasures and sweetness of the Spirit, naught of a truth will be able to heal me, naught will be able to satisfy me. And since this is so :

Surrender thou thyself now completely.

3. Here it is to be noted that any soul that truly loves cannot wish to gain satisfaction and contentment until it truly possess God. For not only do all other things fail to satisfy it, but rather, as we have said, they increase its hunger and desire to see Him as He is. And thus, since each visit that the soul receives from the Beloved, whether it be of knowledge, or feeling, or any other communication soever (which are like messengers that communicate to the soul some knowledge of who He is, increasing and awakening the desire the more, even as crumbs increase a great hunger), makes it grieve at being entertained with so little, the soul says : 'Surrender thou thyself completely.'

4. Since all that can be known of God in this life, much though it be, is not true knowledge for it is knowledge in part and very far off, while to know Him essentially is true knowledge, which the soul begs here, therefore she is not content with these other communications, and says next :

From to-day do thou send me now no other messenger.

5. As though she were to say : Permit me not henceforward to know Thee thus imperfectly through these messengers—to wit, by the knowledge and the feelings that I am given of Thee, so far distant and removed from that which my soul desires of Thee. For to one who grieves for Thy presence, well knowest Thou, my Spouse, that the messengers bring an increase of affliction : for the one reason, because with the knowledge of Thee that they give they re-open the wound ; for the other, because they seem but to delay Thy coming. Wherefore from this day forth do Thou send me no more of such far distant knowledge, for if until now I could make shift with them, since I neither knew Thee nor loved Thee much, now the greatness of the love that I have to Thee cannot be satisfied with this earnest of knowledge : wherefore do Thou surrender Thyself completely. It is as if she said more clearly : This thing, O Lord my Spouse, that Thou art giving of Thyself in part to my soul, do Thou now give completely and wholly. And this thing that Thou art showing as in glimpses, do Thou now show completely and clearly. This that Thou art communicating through intermediaries, which is like to communicating Thyself in mockery, do Thou now communicate completely and truly, giving Thyself through Thyself. For at times in Thy visits it seems that Thou art about to give the jewel of the possession of Thyself, and, when my soul regards it well, she finds herself without it ; for Thou hidest it from her, which is as it were to give it in mockery. Surrender

Thyself, then, completely, giving Thyself wholly to the whole of my soul, that it wholly may have Thee wholly, and be Thou pleased to send me no other messenger.

For they cannot tell me what I wish.

6. As though she were to say : I wish for Thee wholly, and they are unable and know not how to speak to me of Thee wholly ; for naught on earth or in heaven can give the soul the knowledge which she desires to have of Thee, and thus they cannot tell me that which I wish. In place of these messages, therefore, be Thou Thyself messenger and messages both.

THE SHAFT OF LOVE

He speaks of such an extraordinary grace as that enjoyed by St. Teresa, who was as it were pierced with a lance from the hand of a seraph.

No mortal man can know if he be worthy of the grace or of the abomination of God. So that the intent of the soul in this present line is not only to beg for sensible and affective devotion, wherein there is neither certainty nor evidence of the possession of the Spouse in this life by grace, but also to beg for the presence and clear vision of His Essence, wherewith it desires to be given assurance and satisfaction in glory.

3. This same thing was signified by the Bride in the Divine Songs when, desiring union and fellowship with the divinity of the Word her Spouse, she begged the Father for it, saying : *Indica mihi, ubi pascas, ubi cubes in meridie.* Which is to say : Tell me where Thou feedest, and where Thou dost rest at noon. For to enquire of Him where He fed was to beg that she might be shown the Essence of the Divine Word, for the Father glories not, save in the Word, His only Son, neither feeds upon aught else. And to beg Him

to show her where He rested at noon was to beg that self-same thing, since the Father rests not, neither is present in any place, save in His Son, in whom He rests, communicating to Him all His Essence—' at noon,' which is in Eternity, where He ever begets Him. It is this pasture, then, where the Father feeds, and this flowery bed of the Divine Word, where He rests hidden from every mortal creature, that the Bride— the soul—entreats when she says : ' Whither hast Thou hidden Thyself ? '

4. And it is to be observed, if one would learn how to find this Spouse (so far as may be in this life), that the Word, together with the Father and the Holy Spirit, is hidden essentially in the inmost centre of the soul. Wherefore the soul that would find Him through union of love must issue forth and hide itself from all created things according to the will, and enter within itself in deepest recollection, communing there with God in loving and affectionate fellowship, esteeming all that is in the world as though it were not. Hence St. Augustine, speaking with God in the *Soliloquies*, said : ' I found Thee not, O Lord, without, because I erred in seeking Thee without that wert within.' He is, then, hidden within the soul, and there the good contemplative must seek Him, saying : ' Whither hast Thou hidden Thyself ? '

And hast left me, Beloved, to my sighing ?

5. The Bride calls Him ' Beloved,' in order the more to move and incline Him to her prayer, for, when God is loved indeed, He hears the prayers of His lover with great readiness ; and then in truth He can be called Beloved when the soul is wholly with Him and has not its heart set on aught that is outside Him. Some call the Spouse ' Beloved ' when He is not in truth their Beloved, because they have not their heart wholly with Him ; and thus, before the Spouse, their petition is of less effect.

6. And in the words which she then says : ' And hast left me to my sighing,' it is to be observed that the absence of the Beloved is a continual sighing in the heart of the lover, because apart from Him she loves naught, rests in naught and finds relief in naught ; whence a man will know by this if he have indeed love toward God—namely, if he be content with aught that is less than God. To this sighing St. Paul referred clearly when he said : *Nos intra nos gemimus, expectantes adoptionem filiorum Dei.* That is : We groan within ourselves, waiting for the adoption and possession of sons of God. Which is as though he said : Within our heart, where we have the pledge, we feel that which afflicts us—to wit, the absence. This, then, is the sighing which the soul ever makes, for sorrow at the absence of her Beloved, above all when, having enjoyed some kind of sweet and delectable communion with Him, she is left dry and alone.

THE DART OF LOVE

WE know that the heart of St. Teresa was pierced by the dart of a seraph. It is a grace of this kind which the mystical Doctor describes in the *Living Flame of Love.*

But there is another and more sublime way wherein the soul may be cauterized, which is after this manner. It will come to pass that, when the soul is enkindled in this love, although not so perfectly as in the way of which we have spoken (though it is most meet that it should be so with a view to that which I am about to describe), the soul will be conscious of an assault upon it made by a seraph armed with a dart of most enkindled love, which will pierce the soul, as it were an enkindled coal, or, to speak more truly, as a flame, and will cauterize it in a most sublime manner ; and, when it has pierced and cauterized it thus, the flame will rush forth and will rise suddenly and vehemently, even as comes to pass in a furnace or a forge highly heated ; when they stir and poke the fire, the flame becomes hotter and the fire revives, and then the soul is conscious of this wound, with a delight which transcends all description ; for besides being wholly moved by the stirring and the impetuous motion given to its fire, wherein the heat and melting of love is great, the keen wound and the healing herb wherewith the effect of the dart was being greatly assuaged are felt by the soul in the substance of the spirit, even as in the heart of him whose soul has been thus pierced.

Who can speak fittingly of this grain of mustard seed which now seems to remain in the centre of the heart of the spirit, and which is the point of the wound and the delicacy of its delight ?   And the soul feels its love to be increasing and to be growing in strength and refinement to such a degree that it seems to have within it seas of fire which reach to the farthest heights and depths, filling it wholly with love.

Few souls attain to this state, but some have done so, especially those whose virtue and spirituality was to be transmitted to the. succession of their children.   For God bestows spiritual wealth and strength upon the head of a house according as He means his descendants to inherit the first-fruits of the Spirit.

THE SOUL DYING OF LOVE

Therefore it must be known, with regard to the natural dying of souls that reach this state, that, though the manner of their death, from the natural standpoint, is similar to that of others, yet, in the cause and mode of their death there is a great difference. For while the deaths of others may be caused by infirmities or length of days, when these souls die, although it may be from some infirmity, or from old

age, their spirits are wrested away by nothing less
than some loving impulse and encounter far loftier
and of greater power and strength than any in the
past, for it has succeeded in breaking the web and
bearing away a jewel, which is the spirit. And thus
the death of such souls is very sweet and gentle, more
so than was their spiritual life all their life long, for
they die amid the delectable encounters and sublimest
impulses of love, being like to the swan, which sings
most gently when it is at the point of death. For
this reason David said that the death of saints in the
fear of God was precious.

ST. FRANCIS DE SALES

1567–1622

FRANCIS DE SALES belonged to a noble Savoyard family, and was born at Thourens in 1567. He went to school at Annecy and then studied for seven years at the Jesuit college in Paris, where at his own wish he included a course in theology. While there he was tempted to despair by the idea of predestination, but recovered equilibrium before an image of our Lady ' of Deliverance.' When he was twenty-one he went to read law at the university of Padua, but on returning home announced his wish to become a priest. His father opposed the idea, for he had planned a ' good marriage ' for his son, but upon the Bishop of Geneva promising a distinguished benefice, Francis was allowed to be ordained.

In 1594 he went into the Chablais, where Calvinism was rampant, and reclaimed large numbers for the Faith by his energy, knowledge, and, above all, kindness ; he held conferences with the formidable Bèza himself and even had hopes of his conversion. In 1599 he was appointed coadjutor to the Bishop of Geneva, and three years later succeeded him in the see. He was a model bishop, discharging his pastoral office without inter-mission and yet finding time to write. With St. Jane Frances de Chantal, he in 1610 founded the Visitation nuns, primarily for widows and others who are not strong enough to manage the more austere rules.

The influence of St. Francis was far-reaching. He was invited to preach in many dioceses, and often visited Paris, where he was friendly with St. Vincent de Paul, Cardinal de Bérulle, and other holy men of that time, had preached almost daily to crowded congregations. He died at Lyons in 1622, was canonized in 1665, and was proclaimed a doctor of the Church by Pope Pius IX in 1877.

St. Francis de Sales holds a very high place among spiritual writers, his principal works being the *Introduction to the Devout Life* and the *Treatise on the Love of God.* The first, a justly famous book, carries the reader into the realm of infused contemplation, and both had a huge success. He had a gift for presenting spiritual matters clearly and attractively, making plain the most abstruse ideas and allowing his own loveable character to inform all he wrote

TRANSLATIONS : *L'Introduction à la vie dévote. Le traité de l'Amour de Dieu. Sermons. Lettres. Entretiens Spirituels. Introduction to the Devout Life.*

Treatise on the Love of God.

Introduction to the Devout Life. Trans. by Rev. Allan Ross.

Letters to Persons in Religion.

The Spiritual Conferences. Edited under the supervision of Cardinal Gasquet and Dom Benedict Mackey.

(All published by The Newman Press.)

THE RECOLLECTED SOUL

THE PRAYER OF QUIET

THE soul, then, being thus inwardly recollected in God or before God, now and then becomes so sweetly attentive to the goodness of her well-beloved, that her attention seems not to her to be attention, so purely and delicately is it exercised ; as it happens to certain rivers, which glide so calmly and smoothly that beholders and such as float upon them, seem neither to see nor feel any motion, because the waters are not seen to ripple or flow at all. And it is this admirable repose of the soul which the blessed virgin St. Teresa of Jesus names prayer of quiet, not far different from that which she also calls the sleep of the powers, at least if I understand her right.

Even human lovers are content, sometimes, with being near or within sight of the person they love without speaking to her, and without even distinctly thinking of her or her perfections, satiated, as it were, and satisfied to relish this dear presence, not by any reflection they make upon it, but by a certain gratification and repose, which their spirit takes in it. *A bundle of myrrh is my beloved to me, he shall abide between my breasts. My beloved to me, and I to him, who feedeth among the lilies, till the day break, and the shadows retire. Shew me, O thou whom my soul loveth, where thou feedest, where thou liest in the mid-day.* Do you see, Theomitus, how the holy Sulamitess is contented with knowing that her well-beloved is with her, whether in her bosom, or in her gardens, or elsewhere, so she know where He is. And indeed she is the Sulamitess, wholly peaceable, calm and at rest.

Now this repose sometimes goes so deep in its tranquillity, that the whole soul and all its powers fall as it were asleep, and make no movement nor action whatever except the will alone, and even this does no more than receive the delight and satisfaction which the presence of the well-beloved affords. And what is yet more admirable is, that the will does not even perceive the delight and contentment which she receives, enjoying it insensibly, being not mindful of herself, but of Him whose presence gives her this pleasure, as happens frequently when, surprised by a light slumber, we only hear indistinctly what our friends are saying around us, or feel their caresses almost imperceptibly, not feeling that we feel.

However, the soul who in this sweet repose enjoys this delicate sense of the Divine presence, though she is not conscious of the enjoyment, yet clearly shows how dear and precious this happiness is unto her, if one offer to deprive her of it or divert her from it ; for then the poor soul complains, cries out, yea sometimes weeps, as a little child awakened before it has taken its full sleep, who, by the sorrow it feels in being awakened, clearly shows the content it had in sleeping. Hereupon the heavenly shepherd adjures the daughters of Jerusalem, *by the roes and harts of the fields, not to make the beloved awake until she pleases*, that is, to let her awake of herself. No, Theotimus, a soul thus recollected in her God would not change her repose for the greatest goods in the world.

Such, or little different from it, was the quiet of most holy Magdalen, when sitting at her Master's feet she heard His holy word. Behold her, I beseech you, Theotimus, she is in a profound tranquillity, she says not a word, she weeps not, she sobs not, she sighs not, she stirs not, she prays not. Martha, full of business, passes and repasses through the hall : Mary notices her not. And what does this mean—she hearkens? It means that she is there as a vessel of honour, to receive drop by drop the myrrh of sweetness which the lips of her well-beloved distilled into her heart ; and this Divine lover, jealous of this love-sleep and repose of this well-beloved, chid Martha for wanting to awaken her ; *Martha, Martha, thou are careful, and art troubled about many things. But one thing is necessary, Mary hath chosen the best part, which shall not be taken away from her.* But what was Mary's portion or part? To remain in peace, repose, and quiet, near unto her sweet Jesus.

The well-beloved St. John is ordinarily painted, in the Last Supper, not only lying, but even sleeping in his Majesty's bosom, because he was seated after the fashion of the Easterns (*Levantins*), so that his head was towards his dear lover's breast ; and as he slept no corporal sleep there—what likelihood of that?—so I make no question but that, finding himself so near the breasts of the eternal sweetness, he took a profound mystical sleep, like a child of love which locked to its mother's breasts sucks while sleeping. Oh! what a delight it was to this Benjamin, child of his Saviour's joy, to sleep in the arms of that father, who the day after, recommended him, as the Benoni, child of pain, to his mother's sweet breasts. Nothing is more desirable to the little child, whether he wake or sleep, than his father's bosom and mother's breast.

Wherefore, when you shall find yourself in this simple and pure filial confidence with our Lord, stay there, my dear Theotimus, without moving yourself to make sensible acts, either of the understanding or of the will ; for this simple love of confidence, and this love-sleep of your spirit in the arms of the Saviour, contains by excellence all that you go seeking hither and thither to satisfy your taste ; it is better to sleep upon this sacred breast than to watch elsewhere, wherever it be.

THE WOUND OF LOVE

LOVE is the first, yea the principle and origin, of all the passions, and therefore it is love that first enters the heart ; and because it penetrates and pierces down to the very bottom of the will where its seat is, we say it wounds the heart. 'It is sharp,' says the Apostle of France, 'and enters into the spirit most deeply.' The other affections enter indeed, but by the agency of love, for it is this which piercing the heart makes a passage for them. It is only the point of the dart that wounds, the rest only increases the wound and the pain.

Now, if it wound, it consequently gives pain. Pomegranates, by their vermilion colour, by the multitude of their seeds, so close set and ranked, and by their fair crowns, vividly represent, as St. Gregory says, most holy charity, all red by reason of its ardour towards God, loaded with all the variety of virtues, and alone bearing away the crown of eternal reward : but the juice of pomegranates, which, as

we know is so agreeable both to the healthy and to the
sick, is so mingled of sweet and sour that one can
hardly discern whether it delights the taste more
because it has a sweet tartness or because it has a
tart sweetness. Verily, Theotimus, love is thus bitter-
sweet, and while we live in this world it never has the
sweetness perfectly sweet, because it is not perfect,
nor ever purely satiated and satisfied ; and yet it
fails not to be of very agreeable taste, its tartness
correcting the lusciousness of its sweetness, as its
sweetness heightens the relish of its tartness. But how
can this be ? You shall see a young man enter into a
company, free, hearty, and in the best of spirits,
who, being off his guard, feels, before he goes away,
that love, making use of the glances, the gestures,
the words, yea even of the hair of a silly and weak
creature, as of so many darts, has smitten and wounded
his poor heart, so that there he is, all sad, gloomy and
depressed. Why I pray you is he sad ? Without
doubt because he is wounded. And what has wounded ?
Love. But love being the child of complacency, how
can it wound and give pain ? Sometimes the beloved
object is absent, and then, my dear Theotimus, love
wounds the heart by the desire which it excites ;
this it is which, being unable to satiate itself, grievously
torments the spirit.

If a bee had stung a child, it were to poor purpose,
to say to him : Ah ! my child, the bee that stung you
is the very same that makes the honey you are so
fond of. For he might say : It is true, that its honey
is very pleasant to my taste, but its sting is very painful,
and while its sting remains in my cheek I cannot be
at peace, and do you not see that my face is all swollen
with it ? Theotimus, love is indeed a complacency,
and consequently very delightful, provided that it
does not leave in our heart the sting of desire ; for
when it leaves this, it leaves therewith a great pain.
True it is this pain proceeds from love, and therefore

it is a loveable and beloved pain. Hear the painful yet love-full ejaculations of a royal lover. *My soul hath thirsted after the strong living God ; when shall I come and appear before the face of God ? My tears have been my bread day and night, whilst it is said to me daily : Where is thy God ?* And the sacred Sulamitess wholly steeped in her dolorous loves, speaking to the daughters of Jerusalem : *Ah !* says she, *I adjure you, O daughters of Jerusalem, if you find my beloved, that you tell him that I languish with love. Hope that is deferred afflicteth the soul.*

Now the painful wounds of love are of many sorts. (1) The first strokes we receive from love are called wounds because the heart which appeared sound, entire and all its own before its love, being struck with love begins to separate and divide itself from itself, to give itself to the beloved object. Now this separation cannot be made without pain, seeing that pain is nothing but the division of living things which belong to one another. (2) Desire incessantly stings and wounds the heart in which it is, as we have said. (3) But, Theotimus, speaking of heavenly love, there is in the practice of it a kind of wound given by God Himself to the soul which He would highly perfect. For He gives her admirable sentiments of and in-comparable attractions for His sovereign Goodness, as if pressing and soliciting her to love Him ; and then she forcibly lifts herself up as if to soar higher towards her Divine object ; but stopping short, because she cannot love as much as she desires ; O God ! She feels a pain which has no equal. At the same time that she is powerfully drawn to fly towards her dear well-beloved, she is also powerfully kept back and cannot fly, being chained to the base miseries of this mortal life and of her own powerless-ness : she desires *the wings of a dove that she might fly away and be at rest,* and she finds not. There then she is, rudely tormented between the violence of her desires and her own powerlessness. *Unhappy man that*

I am, said one of those who have experienced this torture, *who shall deliver me from the body of this death?* In this case, if you notice, Theotimus, it is not the desire of a thing absent that wounds the heart, for the soul feels that her God is present ; He has already led her into His wine-cellar, He has planted upon her heart the banner of love ; but still, though already He sees her wholly His, He urges her, and from time to time casts a thousand thousand darts of His love, showing her, in new ways, how much more He is loveable than loved. And she, who has not so much force to love as love to force herself, seeing her forces so weak in respect of the desire she has to love worthily Him whom no force of love can love enough—Ah ! she feels herself tortured with an incomparable pain ; for, as many efforts as she makes to fly higher in her desire in love, so many thrills of pain does she receive.

This heart in love with its God, desiring infinitely to love, sees notwithstanding that it can neither love nor desire sufficiently. And this desire which cannot come to effect is as a dart in the side of a noble spirit ; yet the pain which proceeds from it is welcome, because whosoever desires earnestly to love, loves also earnestly to desire, and would esteem himself the most miserable man in the universe, if he did not continue the desire to love that which is so sovereignly worthy of love. Desiring to love, he receives pain ; but loving to desire, he receives sweetness.

My God ! Theotimus, what am I going to say ? The blessed in heaven, seeing that God is still more loveable than they are loving, would fail and eternally perish with a desire to love Him still more if the most holy will of God did not impose upon theirs the admirable repose which it enjoys : for they so sovereignly love this sovereign will, that its willingness stays theirs, and the Divine contentment contents them, they acquiescing to be limited in their love even by that will whose goodness is the object of love.

If this were not so, their love would be equally delicious and dolorous, delicious by the possession of so great a good, dolorous through an extreme desire of a greater love. God therefore continually drawing arrows, if we may say so, out of the quiver of His infinite beauty, wounds the heart of His lovers, making them clearly see that they do not love Him nearly as much as He is worthy to be loved. That mortal who does not desire to love the Divine goodness more, loves Him not enough ; sufficiency in this Divine exercise is not sufficient, when a man would stay in it as though it sufficed him.

ABANDONMENT TO GOD'S PLEASURE

We may well believe that the most sacred Virgin, our Lady, received so much pleasure in carrying her little Jesus in her arms, that delight beguiled weariness, or at least made it agreeable ; for if a branch of *agnus castus* can solace and unweary travellers, what solace did not the glorious mother receive in carrying the immaculate Lamb of God ? And though she permitted Him now and then to run on foot by her, she holding Him by the hand, yet this was not because she would not rather have had Him hanging about her neck and on her breast, but it was to teach Him to form His steps and walk alone. And we ourselves, Theotimus, as little children of the heavenly Father, may walk with Him in two ways. For we may, in the first place, walk with the steps of our own will which we conform to His, holding always with the hand of our obedience the hand of His Divine intention, and following it wheresoever it leads—which is what God requires from us by the significance of His will ; for since He wills me to do what He ordains, He wills me to have the will to do it : God has signified that He wills me to keep holy the day of rest ; since He wills me to do

it, He wills then that I will do it, and for this end
I should have a will of my own, by which I follow
His, conforming myself and corresponding to His.
But we may on other occasions walk with our Saviour
without any will of our own, letting ourselves simply
be carried at His Divine good pleasure, as a little
child in its mother's arms, by a certain kind of consent
which may be termed union or rather unity of our heart
with God's ; and this is the way that we are to endeavour to comport ourselves in God's will of good-
pleasure, since the effects of this will of good-pleasure
proceed purely from His Providence, and we do not
effect them, but they happen to us. True it is we may
will them to come according to God's will, and this
willing is excellent, yet we may also receive the events
of heaven's good-pleasure by a most simple tranquillity
of our will, which, willing nothing whatever, simply
acquiesces in all that God would have done in us,
on us, or by us.

If one had asked the sweet Jesus when He was
carried in His mother's arms, whither He was going,
might He not with good reason have answered : I go
not, 'tis My mother that goes for Me : And if one
had said to Him : But at least do you not go with
your mother ? Might He not reasonably have replied :
No, I do not go, or if I go whither My mother carries
Me, I do not Myself walk with her nor by My own
steps, but by My mother's, by her, and in her. But
if one had persisted with Him, saying : But at least,
O most dear Divine Child, You really will to let
Yourself be carried by Your sweet mother ? No,
verily, might He have said, I will nothing of all this,
but as My entirely good mother walks for Me so she
wills for Me ; I leave her the care as well to go as
to will to go for Me where she likes best ; and as I
go not, but by her steps so I will not, but by her will ;
and from the instant I find Myself in her arms, I give
no attention either to willing or not willing, turning

all other cares over to My mother, save only the care
to be on her bosom, to suck her sacred breast, and to
keep Myself close clasped to her most beloved neck,
that I may most lovingly kiss her with all the kisses
of My mouth. And be it known to you that while I
am amidst the delights of these holy caresses which
surpass all sweetness, I consider that My mother is a
tree of life, and Myself on her as its fruit ; and I am
her own heart in her breast, or her soul in the midst
of her heart, so that as her going serves both her and
Me without My troubling Myself to take a single step,
so her will serves us both without My producing any
act of My will about going or coming. Nor do I ever
take notice whether she goes fast or slow, hither or
thither, nor do I enquire whither she means to go,
contenting Myself with this, that go whither she
please I go still locked in her arms, close laid to her
beloved breasts, where I feed as amongst lilies.   O
Divine Child of Mary ! Permit my poor soul these
outbursts of love : Go then soul, O most amiable
dear little babe, or rather go not, but stay, thus holily
fastened to your sweet mother's breasts. Go always
in her and never be without her whilst thou remainest
a child ! *O how blessed is the womb that bore Thee and
the breasts that gave Thee suck !* The Saviour of our
souls had the use of reason from the instant of His
conception in His mother's womb, and could make all
this discourse ; so could even the glorious St. John,
His forerunner, from the day of the holy Visitation,
and though both of them, as well in that time as all
through their infancy, were possessed of liberty to
will or not to will, yet, in what concerned their external
conduct, they left to their mothers the care of doing
and willing for them what was requisite.

Thus should we be, Theotimus, pliable and tractable
to God's good pleasure, as though we were of wax,
not giving our thoughts leave to wander in wishing
and willing things, but leaving God to will and do

them as He pleases, *throwing upon Him all our solicitude, because He has care of us,* and the holy Apostle says : And note that he says *all our solicitude,* that is as well that which concerns the event, as that which pertains to willing or not willing. For He will have a care of the issue of our affairs, and of willing that which is best for us.

Meanwhile let us affectionately give our attention to blessing God in all His works, after the example of Job, saying : *The Lord gave and the Lord hath taken away, the name of the Lord be blessed!* No, Lord ; I will no events, for I leave You to will them for me at Your pleasure, but instead of willing the events I will bless You because You have willed me. O Theotimus ! what an excellent employment of our will is this, when it gives us the care of willing and choosing the effects of God's good-pleasure in order to praise and thank this good-pleasure for such effects.

A CATALOG OF SELECTED DOVER
BOOKS IN ALL FIELDS OF INTEREST

CONCERNING THE SPIRITUAL IN ART, Wassily Kandinsky. Pioneering work by father of abstract art. Thoughts on color theory, nature of art. Analysis of earlier masters. 12 illustrations. 80pp. of text. 5⅜ x 8½. 23411-8

ANIMALS: 1,419 Copyright-Free Illustrations of Mammals, Birds, Fish, Insects, etc., Jim Harter (ed.). Clear wood engravings present, in extremely lifelike poses, over 1,000 species of animals. One of the most extensive pictorial sourcebooks of its kind. Captions. Index. 284pp. 9 x 12. 23766-4

CELTIC ART: The Methods of Construction, George Bain. Simple geometric techniques for making Celtic interlacements, spirals, Kells-type initials, animals, humans, etc. Over 500 illustrations. 160pp. 9 x 12. (Available in U.S. only.) 22923-8

AN ATLAS OF ANATOMY FOR ARTISTS, Fritz Schider. Most thorough reference work on art anatomy in the world. Hundreds of illustrations, including selections from works by Vesalius, Leonardo, Goya, Ingres, Michelangelo, others. 593 illustrations. 192pp. 7⅛ x 10¼. 20241-0

CELTIC HAND STROKE-BY-STROKE (Irish Half-Uncial from "The Book of Kells"): An Arthur Baker Calligraphy Manual, Arthur Baker. Complete guide to creating each letter of the alphabet in distinctive Celtic manner. Covers hand position, strokes, pens, inks, paper, more. Illustrated. 48pp. 8¼ x 11. 24336-2

EASY ORIGAMI, John Montroll. Charming collection of 32 projects (hat, cup, pelican, piano, swan, many more) specially designed for the novice origami hobbyist. Clearly illustrated easy-to-follow instructions insure that even beginning papercrafters will achieve successful results. 48pp. 8¼ x 11. 27298-2

THE COMPLETE BOOK OF BIRDHOUSE CONSTRUCTION FOR WOOD-WORKERS, Scott D. Campbell. Detailed instructions, illustrations, tables. Also data on bird habitat and instinct patterns. Bibliography. 3 tables. 63 illustrations in 15 figures. 48pp. 5¼ x 8½. 24407-5

BLOOMINGDALE'S ILLUSTRATED 1886 CATALOG: Fashions, Dry Goods and Housewares, Bloomingdale Brothers. Famed merchants' extremely rare catalog depicting about 1,700 products: clothing, housewares, firearms, dry goods, jewelry, more. Invaluable for dating, identifying vintage items. Also, copyright-free graphics for artists, designers. Co-published with Henry Ford Museum & Greenfield Village. 160pp. 8¼ x 11. 25780-0

HISTORIC COSTUME IN PICTURES, Braun & Schneider. Over 1,450 costumed figures in clearly detailed engravings–from dawn of civilization to end of 19th century. Captions. Many folk costumes. 256pp. 8⅜ x 11¾. 23150-X

THE STORY OF THE TITANIC AS TOLD BY ITS SURVIVORS, Jack Winocour (ed.). What it was really like. Panic, despair, shocking inefficiency, and a little heroism. More thrilling than any fictional account. 26 illustrations. 320pp. 5⅜ x 8½.
20610-6

FAIRY AND FOLK TALES OF THE IRISH PEASANTRY, William Butler Yeats (ed.). Treasury of 64 tales from the twilight world of Celtic myth and legend: "The Soul Cages," "The Kildare Pooka," "King O'Toole and his Goose," many more. Introduction and Notes by W. B. Yeats. 352pp. 5⅜ x 8½.
26941-8

BUDDHIST MAHAYANA TEXTS, E. B. Cowell and others (eds.). Superb, accurate translations of basic documents in Mahayana Buddhism, highly important in history of religions. The Buddha-karita of Asvaghosha, Larger Sukhavativyuha, more. 448pp. 5⅜ x 8½.
25552-2

ONE TWO THREE . . . INFINITY: Facts and Speculations of Science, George Gamow. Great physicist's fascinating, readable overview of contemporary science: number theory, relativity, fourth dimension, entropy, genes, atomic structure, much more. 128 illustrations. Index. 352pp. 5⅜ x 8½.
25664-2

EXPERIMENTATION AND MEASUREMENT, W. J. Youden. Introductory manual explains laws of measurement in simple terms and offers tips for achieving accuracy and minimizing errors. Mathematics of measurement, use of instruments, experimenting with machines. 1994 edition. Foreword. Preface. Introduction. Epilogue. Selected Readings. Glossary. Index. Tables and figures. 128pp. 5⅜ x 8½.   40451-X

DALÍ ON MODERN ART: The Cuckolds of Antiquated Modern Art, Salvador Dalí. Influential painter skewers modern art and its practitioners. Outrageous evaluations of Picasso, Cézanne, Turner, more. 15 renderings of paintings discussed. 44 calligraphic decorations by Dalí. 96pp. 5⅜ x 8½. (Available in U.S. only.)   29220-7

ANTIQUE PLAYING CARDS: A Pictorial History, Henry René D'Allemagne. Over 900 elaborate, decorative images from rare playing cards (14th–20th centuries): Bacchus, death, dancing dogs, hunting scenes, royal coats of arms, players cheating, much more. 96pp. 9¼ x 12¼.
29265-7

MAKING FURNITURE MASTERPIECES: 30 Projects with Measured Drawings, Franklin H. Gottshall. Step-by-step instructions, illustrations for constructing handsome, useful pieces, among them a Sheraton desk, Chippendale chair, Spanish desk, Queen Anne table and a William and Mary dressing mirror. 224pp. 8⅛ x 11¼.
29338-6

THE FOSSIL BOOK: A Record of Prehistoric Life, Patricia V. Rich et al. Profusely illustrated definitive guide covers everything from single-celled organisms and dinosaurs to birds and mammals and the interplay between climate and man. Over 1,500 illustrations. 760pp. 7½ x 10⅛.
29371-8